Vivian Khamis

Political Violence and the Palestinian Family
Implications for Mental Health and Well-Being

*Pre-publication
REVIEWS,
COMMENTARIES,
EVALUATIONS . . .*

"**A**n excellent exposé on the suffering of Palestinian families due to political violence. The inherent relationship between violence and human suffering has been documented before, but this is perhaps the most eloquent explanation in the Palestinian context. The victims and the perpetrators alike should read it. While it may help the victims to cope better, it should also make the perpetrators of violence better understand the human dimension of their acts. Hopefully, this book, along with others, will help all of us shape a more peaceful and humane future. I congratulate Dr. Vivian Khamis on her excellent work and recommend the book to all Palestinians and Israelis."

Anwar Islam, PhD
*Associate Professor and Chief,
Health Systems Division,
Department of Community
Health Sciences,
The Aga Khan University,
Pakistan*

More pre-publication
REVIEWS, COMMENTARIES, EVALUATIONS . . .

"**V**ivian Khamis has written a valuable book that in many ways is a pioneering work that fills a glaring gap in the study of Palestinian society. She has skillfully woven quantitative and qualitative research in an effort to unravel the socio-psychological repercussions for Palestinian family life resulting from the recent uprising against Israeli occupation, known as the *Intifada*. By using standard measurement instruments, as well as those that were specifically designed to capture the cultural specificity of Palestinian society, Khamis has added to the academic and professional literature of post-traumatic syndrome. Experiences with trauma and methods of coping are analyzed at the individual and communal level. Khamis does not shy away from depicting the human cost of Israeli occupation and the failure of the Palestinian Authority to ameliorate the effects of violence on Palestinian society. Khamis draws from her study a useful list of policy implications, notably the need to protect human rights as a first measure to safeguard against the use of violence on the civilian population."

Elia Zureik

Professor of Sociology,
Queen's University,
Kingston, Ontario, Canada

HMTP

The Haworth Maltreatment and Trauma Press®
An Imprint of The Haworth Press, Inc.

Political Violence
and the Palestinian Family
Implications for Mental Health and Well-Being

Political Violence
and the Palestinian Family
Implications for Mental Health and Well-Being

Vivian Khamis

HMTP

The Haworth Maltreatment and Trauma Press®
An Imprint of The Haworth Press, Inc.
New York • London • Oxford

Published by

The Haworth Maltreatment and Trauma Press®, an imprint of the The Haworth Press, Inc., 10 Alice Street, Binghamton, NY 13904-1580

Cover design by Jennifer M. Gaska.

Library of Congress Cataloging-in-Publication Data

Khamis, Vivian.
 Political violence and the Palestinian family : implications for mental health and well-being / Vivian Khamis.
  p. cm.
 Includes bibliographical references and index.
 ISBN 0-7890-0898-X (alk. paper) — ISBN 0-7890-1112-3 (pbk. : alk. paper)
  1. Political violence—West Bank—Psychological aspects. 2. Political violence—Gaza Strip—Psychological aspects. 3. Family—Mental health—West Bank. 4. Family—Mental health—Gaza Strip. 5. Intifada, 1987—Psychological aspects. 6. War victims—Mental health—West Bank. 7. War victims—Mental health—Gaza Strip. 8. Palestinian Arabs—Mental health. I. Title.

RC569.5.V55 K43 2000
616.85′82—dc21   99-462145

CONTENTS

Foreword

It is a pleasure for me to write a foreword for Vivian Khamis's book; years ago, she was a student of mine in psychology, and, since then, I have closely followed her research work.

This welcome book is important on many levels: not only does it offer timely and provocative research on political violence and its effect on mental health among Palestinian families, but it also focuses on a sensitive and central area that has long been neglected in psychological literature.

Research from the Arab world is generally scarce in psychological literature; this dearth of research is, however, particularly marked in the field of political violence and its psychological sequelae in an area that has experienced extreme trauma. For many years, Palestinian families have been continuously subjected to various forms of overwhelming oppression, insecurity, and fear; they have been expelled from their homeland, their homes demolished, land expropriated, as well as being harassed, imprisoned, and deported.

To study the effects of trauma-related experiences and their implication for mental health among affected Palestinian families, it is important to note that the discourse on post-traumatic stress disorder (PTSD) is relatively new. The concept emerged in 1980 with the adoption of the DSM-III and the diagnostic category of PTSD, which presented the formulation of posttraumatic reactions in terms of intrusive, constrictive, and hyperarousal symptoms. Most of the data have been generated by studies of Vietnam veterans, and extrapolation to other traumatized populations has not yet been adequately explored. However, the discourse on trauma dates back to the late nineteenth century when the word trauma was extended to include both bodily damage and the psychological manifestation of distressing experiences.

When discussing the field of PTSD among Palestinian families, the centrality of links between the sociopolitical, economic, and psychological fields must be emphasized. One cannot have a discourse on PTSD, trauma, psychiatric symptoms, mental health, and well-being without highlighting the important contextual factors that shape people's experience of, and response to, trauma.

Khamis undertook major sociopsychological research of 900 families affected by the spontaneous popular uprising in the West Bank and Gaza Strip, which started in December 1987 (the *intifada*). This was a significant period in Palestinian "social memory" for its quality of resistance and meaning that evoked national pride and commitment. It was, however, accompanied by prolonged exposure to an array of relentless punitive measures and pervasive traumatic experiences, ranging from loss of life to physical injury, disfigurement, imprisonment, torture, and loss of property.

The families that sustained the *intifada*-related traumas were selected from the Palestinian Human Rights Information Centre 1993 census. These families were divided into four groups: families (1) with one family member who had been killed, (2) with one family member who had been injured, (3) with one family member who had been imprisoned, or (4) whose houses had been demolished. Furthermore, participants, both men and women, represented different age groups, residential areas (urban, rural, or camps), as well as different geographical regions (Gaza Strip, West Bank, and East Jerusalem). Khamis's research methodology combined both the empirically controlled quantitative method and the richness of the qualitative method that draws on human experiences, meanings, and beliefs. She used a battery of scales and questionnaires, conducted in participants' homes, to assess family members' PTSD, psychiatric disorders, stress-related traumas, network and social support resources, coping strategies, ideological commitment (both political and religious), socio-political satisfaction, and well-being.

Discussion by focus groups with moderators formed the basis of her qualitative research. This allowed for understanding of affected families' personal experiences, patterns of behavior, and belief systems. Moderators focused on specific aspects of their traumatic experiences and the variables they associated with their distress and recovery. Participants were randomly selected from the existing database of two agencies, the YMCA and the Ex-detainees Rehabilitation Program. The participants differed in (1) the degree and type of traumas experienced, (2) geographical region, (3) religion, (4) age, (5) sex, (6) education, and (7) employment status. Sixty-four family members were then divided into groups of eight that were homogenous for sex, age, and education.

These two methodological approaches provided a wealth of material concerning the multifaceted nature of political trauma, the ongoing disruptive stressors associated with traumatic events, the closely knit networks that offer differing kinds of support, as well as the belief systems and meanings that sustain the Palestinians' national struggle and strengthen their resilience. The particular features of the Palestinian Arab/Muslim cultural setting provided refuge from the traumatizing coercive policies of Israel.

Khamis's results bring together a rich body of interconnected variables that highlight not only the magnitude and multiplicity of trauma but also the geographic location and certain demographic variables, such as socioeconomic and employment status, as well as gender. Exposure to intense and prolonged trauma was found to have an adverse psychological outcome for a large number of families. The incidence of PTSD was high, and the rate varied with the type and magnitude of the experienced traumatic event. Having a family member killed seems to be a high predictor for the development of PTSD, followed by a family member who had sustained injury or loss of limb, while families with a family member imprisoned seemed to fare better.

Geographic location had a differential effect on family members' mental health outcomes. Families from the densely populated, poverty-stricken Gaza Strip, which had experienced continuous political unrest and violence, showed higher rates of PTSD than those from the West Bank and East Jerusalem. Furthermore, those from a low socioeconomic class, those who were unemployed, older people, and women exhibited the highest rates of PTSD. Here, the contextual factors of people's social, cultural, and political realities seem central. Families' social realities, in terms of their circumstances, available social networks, economic position, and employment status, are important parameters closely associated with the affected family members' mental health. High levels of social support from significant others, from institutions, and from religious and political groups have a complex interaction as buffers for specific strains and certain psychiatric symptoms.

It is evident that in times of crisis people draw on various ideologies, identities, and meaning systems to make sense of who and what they are. The cultural and political reality of Palestinians under prolonged occupation and exposure to various kinds of political violence fostered their search for solace from their harsh conditions and provided them with strength and meaning through political and religious beliefs. Within this belief system, "martyrdom" is acknowledged as a necessary suffering in their legitimate political struggle; their drive to go on and to maintain their national resistance is fueled by their religious belief in *jihad* and *shahadah*. This has allowed them to maintain and endorse their connection to their history and lived values, despite the overwhelming and continuous attempts to undermine their social and cultural ties. Their strong commitment to family, community, and land allows them to go on, although at times the rules that govern family ties and support mechanisms during periods of social transition give way to looser networks that do not offer the same protection. Thus, many women with absent husbands had to shoulder overwhelming responsibilities, often with very limited resources. It is no wonder they suffer more from the psychological effects of such traumas. There is, however, another facet to their reality; having to shoulder the dual responsibilities of caretaker and provider forced many traditional women into the additional roles of political activist and resistance fighter. Although women seem to suffer greater stress that may make them more vulnerable to PTSD or psychological problems such as depression and anxiety, one cannot view their role exclusively in relation to victim status, nor should this obscure the extent of women's contribution to family cohesion and political struggle.

The present social and political reality as perceived by the affected family members revealed an amazing tapestry of themes and narratives in which their suffering, their enormous losses, their harsh existence, their resilience, their pride and commitment to land and country, coupled with their painful disappointment with their present conditions, were intricately woven. Having sustained multiple losses created by traumatic conditions during the military occupation, they are doubly shaken by the unpleasant and, at times, harsh experiences with the new political order. Many Palestinians expressed disappointment and anger at their thwarted hopes and shattered dreams concerning the Palestinian Authority. They have sustained state-sponsored violence for so long and yet continued with their national struggle. However, to suffer injustice, neglect, and victimization by their new Authority is an even harsher reality to face. This, coupled with the debilitating consequences of unemployment, poverty, downward mobility, marginalization, and unmet material and psychological needs, interferes with their posttraumatic adjustment. It is as if the collective distress of these traumatized families has been denied social validation of their suffering and humanity.

Although some research on psychological health has been initiated by Palestinian organizations and human rights institutions in Israel, this research is still embryonic. Khamis's book is valuable as a promising beginning, looking at trauma and its psychological sequelae with a new lens. This will eventually open the doors to a much wider field in which the development of psychological conditions due to political violence are linked to the Palestinians' past, present, and future social worlds. Present reality, whether social, political, or economic, is just a link in a long chain of historical events and experiences. These interlocked links provide the structure for a people's response to political violence and the meaning they give to such events; this will in turn shape how they react and cope with these traumatic events.

When the discourse on trauma due to political violence is more fully explored, all facets and intricacies of the issue need to be highlighted. Future research must acknowledge that trauma discourse cannot be isolated from its constructed reality; hence, one cannot adopt an unqualified approach to the ethnocentric Western discourse on trauma, with its embodied assumptions about suffering and healing, as being universally valid. Each society has its own understanding of suffering, its own subtleties of response, and its own ways of surviving.

Nahid Osseiran
former professor of psychology
American University
Cairo, Egypt

Preface

Political violence is a complex problem with traumatic consequences for victims and their families. A cursory examination of Palestinian history throughout the past fifty years clearly reveals that Palestinians have been subjected to political disasters and oppression that transcend the boundaries of everyday existence. Since the partitioning of Palestine and the creation of the Israeli State in 1948, many Palestinians have been expelled from their homeland, while others have become a minority in Israel. Since the Declaration of Principles in the Oslo accord, signed by the State of Israel and the Palestine Liberation Organization in 1993, approximately 2.5 million Palestinians now live without sovereignty in the West Bank and Gaza Strip. During the *intifada,* the Palestinian popular uprising in the Israeli-occupied West Bank and Gaza Strip that started in December 1987, many Palestinians were killed, injured, imprisoned, deported, and saw their houses demolished. The frequency and diversity of such traumatic events can leave psychological scars and long-lasting effects on the victims and their family members.

This book describes a social psychological study that systematically analyzed the impact of political traumas on the mental health adjustment of the affected family members. In this study, I combined quantitative and qualitative methods of research to ensure that the resulting data would be reasonably comprehensive and useful in guiding successful policy, models of assessment, as well as prevention and intervention programs.

Chapter 1 provides an overview of political victimization. The conceptual issues covered include traumatic events, with an emphasis on political traumas during the *intifada,* trauma-induced stress, role strains, coping, ideology, support resources, socio-political satisfaction, psychological well-being, post-traumatic stress disorder, and psychiatric disorders.

Chapter 2 is organized into two parts that present the methodological framework of the study, including quantitative and qualitative techniques. The first part addresses the methodology of the empirical research, including sampling, procedure, and instrumentation. The second part provides information on the choices and techniques involved in focus groups: designing, conducting, and analyzing.

Chapter 3 is based on the empirical research findings. Topics covered include psychological sequelae of political traumas such as post-traumatic stress disorder (PTSD), psychological well-being, psychiatric disorders, risk factors, and mediators of psychological outcomes following political traumas.

Chapter 4 addresses ten themes that arose in focus group discussions. The themes include several narratives that document victims' experiences and their social suffering. The conclusion for this chapter is well grounded in existing scientific research.

Chapter 5 provides an integrative summary of the major themes contained within the book, in an attempt to signal the future issues and directions of assessment, prevention and treatment, service delivery, legislation and laws, and research in the area of traumatic stress.

Vivian Khamis

Acknowledgments

This research was supported by a grant from the International Development Research Centre (IDRC) in Ottawa, Canada. The generous support of this research center is gratefully acknowledged. Also, the completion of this work was greatly facilitated by the institutional and financial support of the Fulbright program in Washington, DC, Bethlehem University in Palestine, and Harvard University during my sabbatical year as a Fulbright Visiting Scholar in the Department of Psychology at Harvard University. To these institutions I am greatly indebted.

I am especially grateful to the following colleagues and friends for their support and assistance throughout this project: Anwar Islam, IDRC; Elia Zureik, Queens University, Canada; Taisir Abdallah, Bernard Sabella, Eman Abu Sa'da, and Ramsis Ghara, Bethlehem University; and Jumana Odeh, the Palestinian Happy Child Center (PHCC). Thanks are also due to the institutions that accommodated focus groups and to the psychologists and social workers who assisted in data collection.

Most of all my gratitude is to the family members who participated in the research. Their thoughtfulness in describing their lives and their willingness to discuss their experiences, ideas, passion, and suffering are the foundation upon which this work rests.

ABOUT THE AUTHOR

Vivian Khamis is Associate Professor of Psychology and Chair of the Department of Social Sciences, Bethlehem University, Palestine. She has conducted extensive research on traumatic stress and mental health, child maltreatment, psychopathology, and psychosocial problems in Palestine. She is the recipient of numerous awards, including the Fulbright Research Award.

Chapter 1

An Overview of Political Victimization

Since the Israeli occupation of the West Bank and Gaza Strip in June 1967, life for the Palestinians has been characterized by multiple social problems. The onset of the *intifada* in December 1987 added prolonged exposure to a staggering array of extreme political stressors, ranging from relentless punitive measures imposed on the occupants of the territories to the pervasive traumatic experiences of loss of life or limb, loss of freedom (e.g., imprisonment), and loss of property (e.g., demolition of houses). The posttrauma environment brought with it a great upsurge of interest, particularly among psychologists and psychiatrists, in studying the impact of political traumas on Palestinians. Particular attention has been paid to those injured during the *intifada* (Khamis, 1993a,b) and to political prisoners (Sarraj et al., 1996), traumatized women (Khamis, 1998), and families who experienced various forms of political violence (Baker and Kevorkian, 1995; Khamis, 1995a,b). Studies of the injured indicated a high prevalence of post-traumatic stress disorder and low levels of psychosocial adjustment; women and members of affected families suffered from high psychological distress, low subjective well-being, and high levels of anxiety.

The effects of stress associated with major life events and of political stressors on the mental health, psychological well-being, and ongoing life patterns of traumatized Palestinian families have shown that the experience of certain life events, or clusters of these events, can have deleterious effects on subsequent mental health status. However, the nature of the causal connections between such events and subsequent psychiatric disorders has not been established. Previous research (Khamis, 1995a) has limited discussion of life events to how they bear on changes that are primarily personal in nature, and excluded consideration of changes that could be associated with traumatic events or with widespread social processes, such as changes in family roles. Some studies indicated that post-traumatic stress disorder (PTSD) is associated with difficulty in fulfilling family roles (Rosenhech and Thompson, 1986; Solomon, 1988). Specifically, persons with PTSD often experience difficulties with involvement in specific tasks and routines of family life (Maloney, 1988; Solomon, 1988) and marital adjustment (Casella and Motta, 1995). However, most of these studies revolve around interpersonal difficulties in functioning within the family system (Jurich, 1983; Defazio and Pascucci, 1984; Motta, 1990), and they seldom consider factors that mediate the traumatic event-psychological distress relationship.

Despite the enormity of the impact of political violence and the frequency of the problem, few mental health professionals investigated how Palestinian families cope with political traumas. Khamis (1995a,b) examined the Double ABCX model (McCubbin and Patterson, 1983) that regards stressors, family resources, and the family's perception of the situation as three factors that influence adaptation to stress. The results indicated that each of the predictor variables—stressors, resources, coping, and hardiness—contributed to family members' reactions; however, each predictor exhibited a different pattern of relations with the outcome domains. Although coping and support are easily distinguished in principle, they typically co-occur. Furthermore, their effects can be difficult to disentangle. The availability of social support is influential in the prediction of coping behavior and also can facilitate coping strategies by removing some of the distress that can hamper certain coping efforts. Because of the presence of a social network that allows for the provision of support, it can be predicted that people with access to such support will be more likely to seek social support as a coping strategy (Terry, 1991). Similarly, Holahan and Moos (1987) found that individuals with nonsupportive family environments use more avoidance strategies than individuals with high levels of family support. Although perceived availability of social support has been shown to protect individuals from the psychological impact of stressful life events (Cohen and Hoberman, 1983; Cohen and Wills, 1985; Kessler and Mcleod, 1985), an individual's social network also includes conflictive relationships that may be a source of both positive and negative interactions. The negative interactions have been shown to be more consistently and more strongly related to well-being and satisfaction than positive interactions (Fiore, Becker, and Coppel, 1983; Pagel, Erdly, and Becker, 1987; Rook, 1984). Thus, perceived support and quality of relationships appear to be important factors in a complex and interactive stress process including life events, chronic life strains, coping, and social support (Pearlin et al., 1981).

Central to research into coping is an additional factor that might also have a direct effect on the coping process of families of those suffering political traumas: ideology in its political and religious forms (Khamis, 1995a, 1998). Ideology can play an important role in the prediction of behavior. In Lazarus and Folkman's (1984) stress and coping theory, two processes, cognitive appraisal and coping, are identified as critical mediators of stressful person-environment relationships and their immediate and long-term outcomes. Cognitive appraisal is a process in which the person evaluates whether a particular encounter with the environment is relevant to his or her well-being, and if so, in what way (Folkman et al., 1986). There are two kinds of cognitive appraisal: primary and secondary. In primary appraisal, the person evaluates whether he or she has anything at stake in this encounter. Commitment, goals, and beliefs about oneself and the world help to define the stakes that the person identifies as having relevance to well-being in specific stressful transactions. Lazarus and Folkman

(1984) report that commitments and beliefs influence appraisal by shaping the person's understanding of the event, and, in consequence, his or her emotions and coping efforts. Conversely, ideology may dispose the person to cope with political traumas in certain ways that either impair or facilitate the various components of posttrauma recovery. However, although commitment was found to be a vulnerable factor in psychological stress (Bergman and Magnusson, 1979; Fiore, 1979), it could also impel a person toward a course of action that could reduce the threat and help sustain coping efforts in the face of obstacles. In secondary appraisal, the person evaluates what, if anything, can be done to overcome or prevent harm, or to improve the prospects for benefit. Various coping options are evaluated, such as changing the situation, accepting it, seeking more information, or holding back from acting impulsively (Lazarus and Folkman, 1984; Folkman et al., 1986).

Another dimension that might have an impact on the well-being of affected family members is sociopolitical satisfaction, which reflects the quality of life of the people. The ecocultural context of a family is important in determining a person's subjective experience. In fact, the degree of satisfaction experienced is not determined by the absolute value of an event but rather by its value in relation to other contextual events, such as the political situation, work, and social life. Therefore, the quality of life in Palestinian society depends on more than a relative dearth of identifiable problems. As Zatura (1978, p. 8) states, "Freedom from symptoms, although important, is not the only kind of freedom, and the relative absence of pain is not the only source of happiness."

Drawing on all these theoretical viewpoints on coping with traumatic stress, this research investigates the psychological sequelae of political traumas in Palestinian families. In the following section, I will review variables used in the analysis that represent psychosocial processes occuring in the immediate ecocultural context of victims who have been subjected to various forms of political oppression during the *intifada*.

CONCEPTUAL ISSUES IN TRAUMATIC STRESS

Traumatic Events

A traumatic event is conceptualized in the 1994 edition of the *Diagnostic and Statistical Manual of Mental Disorders* (DSM-IV) of the American Psychiatric Association as a person's exposure to an extreme traumatic stressor involving direct personal experience of an event that includes actual or threatened death, serious injury, or other threats to one's physical integrity; witnessing an event that involves death, injury, or a threat to the physical integrity of another person; or learning about unexpected or violent death, serious harm, or threat of death or injury experienced by a family member or other close associate (p. 424).

Among events that meet the stressor criteria of the DSM-IV are those associated with political violence. The Palestinian Human Rights Information Centre estimates that during the period of the *intifada* from December 9, 1987, to December 31, 1993, Palestinians suffered 130,472 injuries and 1,282 deaths, of which 332 were deaths of children. Among these victims are those who were shot, beaten, teargassed, or burned to the extent that they are suffering from permanent disability. Records also show that over 22,088 people were imprisoned, 481 were deported, and 2,532 had their houses demolished during the *intifada*. The psychosocial and financial costs for the affected families in terms of medical and psychosocial care, loss of productive time, chronic disability, loss of function, and loss of life and property are enormous (Khamis, 1995a).

While early disaster and traumatic stress research tended to present a unitary view of trauma, there is increasing recognition of multiple stressor dimensions and that each may be identified by multiple quantitative parameters, such as severity, duration, and potential for recurrence (Raphael and Wilson, 1993). Dohrenwend and Dohrenwend (1974) point out that the multiplicity and periodic recurrence of traumatic events are far more stressful than a single one-time traumatic event (p. 812).

Many Palestinian families have suffered the occurrence of a number of traumatic events simultaneously or within a short time. Also, a number of adverse stressor parameters characterize the political traumas experienced by Palestinian families. For example, a threat to life and limb has been more stressful than threat of loss of freedom (e.g., imprisonment) or even loss of property (e.g., demolition of houses) (Khamis, 1995b).

These traumatic events, by definition, have the potential to raise the family's level of stress. Anything that changes some aspect of the system, such as boundaries, structures, goals, processes, roles, or values, can produce stress (McKenry and Price, 1994).

When a family is in a state of crisis, it does not function adequately. Family boundaries are no longer maintained, customary roles and tasks are no longer performed, and family members are no longer functioning at optimal physical or psychological levels (Boss, 1988). A clearer understanding of the relation of political traumatic events to psychological distress and family functioning requires examining specific stressors, such as role strains.

Role Strains

Role strains are the hardships, challenges, conflicts, or other problems that people come to experience as they engage over time in normal social roles (Pearlin, 1983). These strains, in turn, stand as potentially powerful antecedents of stress and its emotional and physical manifestations. A variety of strains may be experienced by people in the context of their ordinary social roles (Hirsch and Rapkin, 1986; Goode, 1960), such as those generated by multiple roles, inter- and intrarole conflicts, role captivity, loss and gain of roles, and role restructuring (Pearlin, 1983).

Evidence from research (Pearlin and Lieberman, 1979; Pearlin et al., 1981; Brown and Harris, 1978) shows that events can create stress by adversely altering or intensifying the more enduring aspects of key social roles. However, role strain as a response of the family to the demands experienced as a result of a traumatic event has been given little attention in the literature. This response denotes something different from the routine changes within a system that are expected as part of its normal, everyday operation.

Two major hypotheses have been proposed concerning the relation of role involvement to psychological well-being. The "scarcity" hypothesis (Marks, 1977; Goode, 1960) assumes that the social structure normally creates overly demanding role obligations and more cumulative intrarole conflict. Responsibility for multiple roles also opens the door to interrole conflict, involving potentially incompatible demands of individuals across life domains (e.g., spouse versus employer). Moreover, there may simply be too many tasks to perform, leading to role overload (Hirsch and Rapkin, 1986). Because human energy is limited, psychological well-being is impaired by the overload and conflict inherent in numerous, often incompatible roles.

In contrast to this view, the "enhancement" hypothesis (Marks, 1977; Sieber, 1974) emphasizes the benefits rather than the costs of multiple-role involvement: status, privileges, increased self-esteem. However, Pearlin (1983) indicates that whether or not the objective features of roles are transformed into role strains often depends on the dispositions people bring with them to their roles.

Although major social life transitions that are part of life under trauma (e.g., role reversals or dual responsibilities) may tax family members' psychological well-being (Khamis, 1995b), without a doubt there are people for whom the consequences of these role strains are more benign. From this perspective, it is not a question of whether the positive or negative model is correct, but a question of the conditions under which different outcomes occur (Long and Porter, 1984; Stryker, 1980). Therefore, considerable attention should be devoted to the investigation of strategies that might reduce multiple-role stressors as well as various factors that may affect the mental health and psychological well-being of those who experience role strains in Palestinian families.

Coping

Coping strategies are the constantly changing cognitive and behavioral efforts to manage external and/or internal demands that are appraised as taxing or exceeding the resources of the person (Lazarus and Folkman, 1984). This construct has received considerable attention in the psychological literature (e.g., Billings and Moos, 1981; Folkman and Lazarus, 1980; Lazarus, 1981; Pearlin and Schooler, 1978), most frequently as a factor that mediates the relation between stress and physical or mental disorders.

Coping responses are classified in many ways. Pearlin and Schooler (1978) differentiate between efforts to change the situation and attempts to control distress, as well as responses that alter the cognitive appraisal of stress. Billings and Moos (1981) suggest a related typology consisting of active-behavioral strategies, active-cognitive strategies, and avoidance strategies. Lazarus and Folkman (1984) describe two forms of coping: problem-focused strategies that are directed toward the management of a problem and emotion-focused strategies that are directed toward amelioration of the associated level of emotional distress.

In several different studies, problem-focused strategies have been reported to have positive association with well-being (Folkman et al., 1986). A reliance on emotion-focused strategies, on the other hand, tends to be associated with poor mental health (Aldwin and Revenson, 1987; Terry, 1991). However, previous research (e.g., Folkman and Lazarus, 1980, 1985) has shown that people use both forms of coping in virtually every type of stressful encounter. The efficacy of problem- and avoidance-focused coping strategies is also thought to be situationally contingent (Folkman et al., 1986). Emotion-focused coping is believed to be particularly useful in situations in which the source of threat cannot be influenced, whereas problem-focused coping is thought to be most effective in situations in which threat can be altered. For example, in the families of the killed, reliance mainly on emotion-focused coping may be considered effective and appropriate, since not much can be done. In contrast, in the case of families of the injured, resorting to emotional discharge would not be appropriate as a substitute for the direct action of seeking professional help. Thus, the presence and type of specific political traumas may create or promote specific coping strategies.

Recent research has focused on the identification of variables that may influence the type of coping strategies that an individual chooses to adopt in a particular stressful situation (Holahan and Moos, 1987; Terry, 1991, 1994). The results of the studies indicate that stable and situational variables are important. Lazarus and Folkman (1984) view the way in which persons cope as determined in part by their resources, which include existential beliefs, commitments, social support, and personal resources, as well as constraints that mitigate the uses of resources. Personal constraints include internalized cultural values and beliefs that proscribe certain ways of behaving and psychological deficits.

The study of the mechanisms through which coping may be related to outcomes has been approached from several directions. Characteristics of the personality such as fatalism and inflexibility were identified by Wheaton (1983), whereas hardiness was identified by Kobasa (1979). Others focused on the characteristics of the stressful situations (Shanan, De-Nour, and Garty, 1976). Pearlin and Schooler (1978) considered the relative contributions of mastery, self-esteem, and self-denigration and the ways in which people cope with chronic role strains in relation to the amelioration of stress in four role areas: marriage, parenting, household economics, and role occupation. A number of studies have pointed to an association between sociodemographic factors and reliance on certain coping strategies (Billings and Moos, 1981, 1984; Hann, 1977; Menaghan, 1983; Pearlin and Schooler, 1978). However, the empirical results concerning this issue have been mixed (McCrae, 1982).

Outcome variability in terms of coping with trauma in Palestinian families may be explained by various factors, such as sociodemographics, social support, ideology, and sociopolitical satisfaction. The importance of considering various moderators accords with Pearlin's (1993) conception of the stress process, which proposes that coping is best understood when viewed within the larger context of the stress process.

Ideology

Ideology is conceptualized as a generalized attitude with a symbolic basis that is characterized by the expression of politico-religious beliefs and values relevant to self and identity. It represents long-standing commitment to politicoreligious principles and choices, commitment to religion as faith and practice (laws and legislation), and attitudes about the political party (sense of belief, trust, and affiliation).

Palestinians' understanding and experience of political traumas has been colored by their religious and political beliefs and practices. Parsons (1957) claims that "from the psychological point of view, religion has its greatest relevance to the points of maximum strain and tension" (p. 385). Accounts of lives of affected Palestinian families provide support for the role of ideology in sustaining life under the most devastating of circumstances. For example, "martyrdom" is acknowledged as legitimate "suffering" among the majority of Palestinian families. Khamis (1995b) anticipates that this religious ideology might have an impact on a family's assimilation and accommodation to the political traumas caused by the killing of a family member. This is apparent in the funeral of a young "martyr," which is usually celebrated as his wedding.

The mother is often asked to ululate and dance for the "martyrdom" of her son. As Bakan (1968) indicates, suffering for a reason is easier to endure than suffering without cause, benefit, or meaning. It seems that people are strengthened and sustained by their political beliefs and their religious principles that call for *jihad,* holy war, and *shahadah,* martyrdom. This concept of ideology must be introduced to explain phenomena in Palestinian society that cannot be explained by a simple stress-strain model.

Little psychological research has been conducted on ideology per se. However, similar constructs have received considerable attention. Antonovsky (1979) uses the term "generalized resistance resource" to describe characteristics that facilitate the management of stress. These characteristics can be physical, biochemical, artifactual, material, cognitive, emotional, attitudinal, interpersonal, or macrosociocultural. Lazarus and Folkman (1984) are concerned with the resources (e.g., existential beliefs, commitment) that a person draws on to cope. The difference in orientation is reflected in Antonovsky's conception of resources as buffers of stress, whereas Lazarus and Folkman see resources as factors that precede and influence coping, which, in turn, mediate stress. Drawing on these studies, ideology may be explained in two ways: as a buffer of stress or as a factor that mediates stress by influencing the coping process.

Support Resources

The support network in Palestinian communities stresses reliance on the family. Palestinians tend to believe in protecting family members and solving their own problems within their own families and are reluctant to expose personal problems to members outside this group. Extended family relationships, particularly sibling ties, tend to be fairly strong. However, effects of migration and modernization have contributed to the transition of Palestinian society from cultural alienation to cultural integration, which has resulted in new patterns of family interactions. Also, political violence has often resulted in separation from family members and friends (Khamis, 1995a,b; Zureik, Graff, and Ohan, 1990), which can reduce available support networks. However, the experience of harm and pain has influenced Palestinian lives, often resulting in the dismantling and reconstruction of extended familial and communal networks as well as the establishment of support from both religious and political groups.

Support resources constitute those interactions and support which meet psychosocial as well as instrumental needs of the person and are of two types: informal and formal. Informal support is received from immediate family members, collateral relatives, and friends, whereas formal support is received from professional services networks, religious groups, and political organizations.

In defining the construct, Lazarus and Folkman (1984) see resources as what an individual "draws on in order to cope," and they argue that resources "precede and influence coping" (p. 158). Similarly, Thoits (1986) views social support as a source of coping assistance. For example, advice and encouragement from a confidant may increase the likelihood that a person will rely on logical analysis, information seeking, or active problem solving. Holahan and Moos (1987) find that individuals with more personal and social resources are more likely to rely on approach coping and less likely to use avoidance coping. In turn, a higher proportion of approach relative to avoidance coping mediates between family support and healthy outcomes during times of stress (Holahan and Moos, 1990, 1991). Although numerous studies show that social support is linked to positive health outcomes (Cutrona, 1989), researchers (Rook, 1984) emphasize the importance of assessing the content of social relations.

Although there is agreement that social support and intense kin relationships are highly supportive and facilitate postdisaster recovery among victims (Cormie and Howell, 1988; Perry and Lindell, 1978; United Nations Disaster Relief Coordinator [UNDRO]

1986), little empirical evidence is available in this regard. McFarlane (1988) indicates that lack of social support is not associated with greater psychological impairment. With regard to the injured of the *intifada,* Khamis (1993a) argues that the severity of the trauma was so intensely overwhelming that the efficacy of social support was overshadowed. She notes, however, that the importance of social support to mental health varied systematically across outcome measures (i.e., psychosocial adjustment and PTSD), suggesting that social support may affect those processes involved in psychosocial adjustment, without appreciably reducing the arousal associated with stress. In a similar vein, Khamis (1995a) argues that the presence of a trauma in Palestinian families may have reduced resources and, as a result, may have failed to fulfill expectations for aid. According to the theory of reciprocity, a feeling of independence requires reciprocal give and take (Eranen and Liebkind, 1993), which suggests that the inability to repay may make reciprocity difficult. Thus, relying on one's family for support when the family itself is in crisis and in need of support can place an enormous burden on that family. Because all family members are hurt and under great pressure, they may become less able to fulfill one another's needs. Since perceptions of support were influenced by stable individual differences such as gender and age, other personality traits may reflect differences in perceptions of availability under achieved social support. For example, a person's ideology may affect the immediate actual ecocultural niche by resulting in the creation of more support resources from a social network (e.g., political parties or religious groups).

Consequently, a priority in support resources research is the gaining of a better understanding of factors that promote social network transactions, of the role of support resources in stress resistance and its influence on coping strategies, and the effects of support resources on various mental health outcomes.

Sociopolitical Satisfaction

Sociopolitical satisfaction may be conceived as the extent of a person's subjective gratification with the sociopolitical context that confers quality of life. It includes delivery of welfare assistance, social security, political safeness and optimism, personal growth and worth, and rewards obtained in occupation.

Several sociopsychological concepts, such as self-esteem, locus of control, depression, or alienation, tap aspects of the quality of life indirectly, but only satisfaction has a "bottom-line" finality in terms of consequences for the individual (Andrews and Robinson, 1991). Also, some of the most powerful statistical predictors of global well-being have proven to be assessments of specific life concerns, such as evaluations of family, housing, job, or community (Andrews and Withey, 1976; Campbell, Converse, and Rodgers, 1976; Michalos, 1980, 1983; Zapf and Glatzer, 1987). To date, several perceived functions, conditions, or services have been identified as important in determining life satisfaction (White, 1985). Some of these are availability and adequacy of interpersonal relations and social supports (Bardo, 1976; Widgery, 1982); availability of recreational, educational, medical, and employment service opportunities (Rojek, Clemente, and Summers, 1975); perceived security (Marans and Rodgers, 1975); and perceived control over community affairs (Bardo, 1976; Goudy, 1977). Indeed, the literature on satisfaction with the quality of life seems to be more informative about perceived characteristics that interfere with subjective well-being (Diener and Diener, 1995) than about sociopolitical satisfaction that facilitates coping. However, if we assume that adequacy of support and the efficacy of coping strategies are all tapping into that attribute of human experience called sense of well-being, indicators of sociopolitical satisfaction would still correlate most highly with subjective well-being in Palestinian families who sustained political traumas.

The losses resulting from a traumatic event (e.g., death, injury) clearly have the capacity to create certain effects on the way a person evaluates his or her life. These unpredictable catastrophes make it difficult to predict well-being from a knowledge of the more stable attributes of the person. In fact, the phenomenal rise in ideology (e.g., religious and political) has moved a substantial portion of the Palestinian population beyond the point at which their lives are dominated by the elemental problems of sheer survival and has created a more introspective view of specific life concerns. The implicit causal assumption underlying all these analyses is that predictors of sociopolitical satisfaction are related to personality characteristics such as ideology, and to a person's appraisal of the traumatic event and the associated stressors that it entails. Also, subjective well-being is related to a person's evaluative reactions to his or her sociopolitical life, either in terms of its direct effect or its influence on coping strategies.

Well-Being

Psychological well-being (PWB) is an attitude that includes people's cognitive and affective evaluations of their lives (Diener and Larsen, 1993; Myers and Diener, 1995).

An examination of the emerging literature on stress shows a linkage between normative stressors and psychological well-being (Mitchell and Hodson, 1986; Vanfossen, 1986), giving less attention to the impact of traumatic events such as political violence. Research on families who have been subjected to political violence has focused on psychosomatic illnesses (Hadden and McDevitt, 1974; Parkes, 1977), psychiatric disorders (Allodi, 1980), and post-traumatic stress disorder (Wilson, 1988, 1989).

Individual differences in psychological well-being have also been related to demographic and social classification variables (Andrews and Withey, 1976; Davis, Fine-Davis, and Meehan, 1982; Michalos, 1985), personality variables (Costa and McCrae, 1980; Emmons and Diener, 1985), social support (Mitchell and Hodson, 1986;

Vanfossen, 1986), and evaluation of specific life concerns (Andrews and Withey, 1976; Davis, Fine-Davis, and Meehan, 1982).

Psychological well-being differs not only in the nature of people's subjective experiences but also in the types of appraisals and interpretations that precede or elicit them (e.g., Ortony, Clore, and Collins, 1988; Roseman, 1991). For example, it is generally agreed that sadness is associated with the perception of loss, that anger is associated with the perception of goals being blocked, and that blame is attributed to others (Berenbaum, Fujita, and Pfennig, 1995; Emmons, 1986; Lazarus and Folkman, 1984). Therefore, one would expect individual differences in psychological well-being to be associated with individual differences in cognitive styles or schemata, such as the types of attitudes or beliefs an individual holds and the type of attributions he or she makes (Berenbaum, Fujita, and Pfennig, 1995) regarding specific behaviors of supportive individuals.

Psychiatric Symptomatology

Psychological responses of survivors of political violence are protean. They include impaired memory and concentration, mood disorders, headaches, anxiety, depression, sleeplessness due to nightmares and other intrusive phenomena, emotional numbing, sexual disturbances, rage, social withdrawal, lack of energy, apathy, and helplessness (Allodi, 1980; Allodi and Cowgill, 1982; Khamis, 1995a,b; Westermeyer and Williams, 1998).

The notion that an extreme traumatic event produces a pure case of post-traumatic stress disorder is somewhat of a rarity. PTSD often occurs in conjunction with other affective disorders, particularly anxiety and depression (Scott and Stradling, 1993). The symptoms that can accompany anxiety and depression may be categorized under four headings: thoughts, feelings, behaviors, and psychological effects (Beck, Emery, and Greenberg, 1985).

Although the psychological effects of political violence have been investigated (Goldfeld et al., 1988; Khamis, 1993a,b,

1995a,b, 1998), there are few controlled studies of its psychological impact (Paker, Paker, and Yuksel, 1992).

Although most studies concur about the nature of the psychological problems in the short and long term following a disaster, the question of whether these problems are independent of confounding variables, such as other associated traumatic events before and after the initial traumatic event, has thus far not been fully resolved. Smith and North (1993) indicate that rates of diagnosable disorders are generally low after disasters; however, symptoms are plentiful. That symptoms abound but do not cluster into diagnosable syndromes within the current system of psychiatric classification might suggest that syndromes may actually cluster into some, as yet undefined, grouping. Also, the results of the studies are inconsistent regarding the effect of the type of trauma (Madakasira and O'Brien, 1987; McFarlane, 1986; Parker, 1977) and demographics (Fairley, 1984; Gleser, Green, and Winget, 1981; Lopez-Ibor, Canas, and Rodriguez-Gamazo, 1985; Madakasira and O'Brien, 1987).

Since each disaster event and each affected community have unique characteristics, it is worthwhile to examine the degree to which psychiatric disorders differ with individual dispositional variables such as age, gender, and level of education; situational variables such as coping strategies, social support, and ideology; and trauma-related variables such as the type of trauma. This will shed light on macrosocial variables that influence mean levels of psychiatric disorders.

Post-Traumatic Stress Disorder

In the DSM-IV (American Psychiatric Association, 1994), post-traumatic stress disorder (PTSD) is classified as an anxiety disorder and is characterized by the reexperiencing of an extremely traumatic event, accompanied by symptoms of increased arousal and by avoidance of stimuli associated with the trauma.

The diagnostic criteria for PTSD include reliving the trauma, emotional numbing, disturbances in interpersonal relations, and a variety of autonomic symptoms such as sleep disturbance and hyperarousability.

PTSD has occupied a central place in psychiatric research. Many of the data have been generated from investigations of American Vietnam War veterans (Wilson, 1988, 1989). This raises many questions about the extent to which the findings can be extrapolated to other populations, such as the Palestinians, just as it is difficult to generalize from any studies of disaster (Green and Grace, 1988).

Since the onset of the *intifada* in December 1987, there has been a steady increase in the intensity and frequency of political violent acts against the Palestinians that presumably has taxed their mental health and well-being (Khamis, 1993a,b, 1995a,b, 1998). Although the psychological sequelae to traumatic events have become recognized as comprising post-traumatic stress disorders (American Psychiatric Association, 1994), only a few published studies have examined PTSD among Palestinians (Khamis, 1993a; Sarraj et al., 1996). They focused on the impact of political traumas on direct victims such as the injured and political prisoners. However, studies on the impact of political violence on the Palestinian family unit are almost nonexistent. This being so, a pressing need exists for a better understanding of the impact of political traumas on the family in a typical developing country such as Palestine.

Since PTSD is a recent diagnostic entity that is still evolving, and there is little uniformity in the methodology across studies, and since each disaster event and each affected community has unique characteristics (Smith and North, 1993), further research will help clarify these definitional problems and ambiguities, especially as related to identification of factors that promote or inhibit PTSD.

Chapter 2

Methodology

A number of issues have plagued the research of the psychological sequelae of political traumas. Generally, individual biases and ideological differences reside in the very methodological approaches that are advised by various researchers. However, the methodology employed by previous Palestinian studies in this domain has used quantitative approaches as opposed to qualitative approaches. From a clinical perspective, the limitations of specific and quantifiable responses are that they fail to enlighten our knowledge about the processes underlying the traumatic experience and, at a subjective level, to provide insights into the feelings, passions, and sufferings of the traumatized people. By the same token, the qualitative techniques lack the representativeness of a much larger inferential population that quantitative methods obtain through random sampling methods.

To capitalize on the strengths and minimize the weaknesses of each method (Maton, 1993; Hines, 1993), this study provides a conceptual and methodological framework with a cultural perspective, whereby the quantitative methods of survey research are linked with the methods derived from a qualitative ethnographic approach. Quantitative methodologies emphasize empiricism and hypothesis testing and are most closely associated with the "etic" perspective, which considers phenomena in relation to predetermined concepts and hypotheses, often in isolation from the context in which they occur. The standardization of data collection procedures is emphasized, issues to be explored are determined a priori, and categories for responding are supplied by the researcher rather than the respondent. The influence of the observer on the research process is reduced through the use of assessment tools with known validity and reliability (Hughes, Seidman, and Williams, 1993).

In contrast, qualitative research provides what anthropologists refer to as an "emic" perspective of a group's experience. The utility of understanding phenomena from the perspective of group members is emphasized, allowing it to emerge within the context of the researcher's interaction with the group. Importance is placed on understanding the group's patterns of behavior and systems of meaning in naturalistic settings, emphasizing understanding social processes rather than predicting outcomes. Preconceived rules and categories for classifying behavior are deemphasized, and the analysis of data is inductive (Hughes, Seidman, and Williams, 1993).

Therefore, the overall research plan for the study called for an initial period of empirical field research, to be followed by focus group discussions. The design reflects the twofold objectives: (1) the quantitative analysis was concerned with the relative contribution of trauma-related variables, individual dispositional variables, and contextual variables in accounting for variations in psychological well-being, psychiatric disorders, and post-traumatic stress disorders of Palestinian family members who sustained *intifada*-related traumas, and (2) the qualitative approach encouraged ideas to emerge from the groups in regard to what the participants themselves would consider important variables that could account for family distress. The goal was to gain reactions to areas needing improvement, and to set general guidelines for how an intervention might operate and how a social policy is reinforced.

The following sections will present the methods and techniques that were employed in the study. The first section will include sampling, data collection techniques, and statistical treatment of the data. The second section will be devoted to the mechanics of designing, conducting, and interpreting the outcomes of focus groups conducted in this study.

PART I: QUANTITATIVE STUDY

Sample Selection

The design for sample selection was based on four primary stratified variables: type of trauma, gender, geographic region, and residential pattern. Data from the 1993 Palestinian Human Rights Information Centre (PHRIC) census were used to allocate Palestinian families who sustained *intifada*-related traumas.

Members of affected families were categorized in four groups, each of equal number, namely, families with one member who had been (1) killed, (2) injured, or (3) imprisoned, and (4) families whose houses had been demolished. However, as the interviewing progressed, the distribution of the type of trauma within the predetermined subgroups became unequal. This was due to the multiple traumatic dimensions that arose in association with the primary traumas selected from the PHRIC records.

The design also called for proportional representation of geographic regions—the West Bank, Gaza Strip, and East Jerusalem—as well as various residential patterns (i.e., city, village, and camp). In addition, the sample included both sexes and a variety of family roles (e.g., wives, husbands, or parents). If a selected person was unavailable or unable to participate, a second-choice family member with similar characteristics was asked to participate.

Participants

The sample size was 900, of whom 463 (51.4 percent) were men and 437 (48.6 percent) women. From this sample, 63 (7 percent) were identified as having a family member killed; 72 (8 percent) injured; 130 (14.5 percent) imprisoned; 29 (3.2 percent) as having a house demolished; and 606 (67.3 percent) as having undergone more than one traumatic event. They ranged in age from twenty-five to seventy years ($M = 47.20$, $SD = 12.44$). Of the sample, 810 (90 percent) were married, 600 (66.7 percent) had a preparatory school education or less, while 300 (33.3 percent) had secondary education or some college.

The combined monthly income of the participants' families ranged from 60 to 1,500 U.S. dollars ($M = 670$, $SD = 804$). Most were housewives (351, or 39 percent); 190 (21.1 percent) were unemployed; 177 (19.7 percent) were laborers; 96 (10.7 percent) held service, technical, and sales occupations; 47 (5.2 percent) teachers; and 39 (4.3 percent) in farm work. The majority were Muslims (876, or 97.3 percent); 24 (2.7 percent) were Christians. Geographically, 598 (66.4 percent) were from the West Bank, 249 (27.7 percent) from the Gaza Strip, and 53 (5.9 percent) from Jerusalem, representing various residential patterns: 287 (31.9 percent) from refugee camps, 346 (38.4 percent) from urban areas, and 267 (29.7 percent) from rural areas.

Procedure

Informed consent was obtained from 98 percent of the participants who were selected to participate in the study. They were given a full explanation of the study, were assured of the anonymity of their responses, and were ensured confidentiality of all information collected. Interviews, which generally lasted from one to two hours, were conducted by four trained interviewers in the participants' homes. These interviewers were social workers or psychologists who had previously participated in field studies.

Pilot Study

A total sample of 150 family members was selected from PHRIC to participate in a pilot study. The criteria used to choose participants for inclusion in the pilot study were similar to those used for the sample selection for the quantitative study. The purposes of the pilot study were to obtain data on the factorial composition of the instruments and their intercorrelations, to determine the internal consistency of each instrument, and to obtain data on the difficulty and discrimination of each instrument item.

Following data collection, each interviewer was asked to evaluate the items and materials, to list any problems in conducting the interviews, and to summarize the participants' reactions to each instrument.

Instrumentation

The measures in this study were administered as a battery of questionnaires focusing on trauma-induced stress, stressors and mental health consequences, as well as risk factors and mediators of psychological outcomes following political traumas. Most of the scales reported in this section have been constructed for the purpose of this study to capture the peculiarities of the Palestinian people in enduring, recovering from, and succumbing to political traumas. The statements of these scales were generated from previous observations and interviews of inflicted family members who had suffered political traumas, and from a review of related theoretical and empirical research. Also, four specialists in the areas of psychology, psychiatry, and the Palestinian society were asked to judge the overall format of the scales and to assess each scale item for its presumed relevance to the property being measured. Only statements that were unanimously agreed upon were used, which reinforced the validity of the scales. However, the assessment of PTSD and psychiatric symptomatology have been adopted and adapted due to the universality of the characteristic symptoms (Blake, Albano, Keane, 1992; Joseph, Williams, and Yule, 1997).

Family Data Sheet

This brief questionnaire secured demographic and background information about family members, including the direct victim. The respondents' sociodemographics were gender, level of education completed, religion, marital status, employment, residential pattern (urban, rural, and refugee camps), number of children, and total household income. The trauma-related questions included type of political trauma exposure, such as having a family member killed, injured, or imprisoned, or having their houses demolished. Also, respondents were asked if they were subjected to other forms of traumatic events or social problems.

Post-Traumatic Stress Disorder

Post-traumatic stress disorder was assessed by using the diagnostic criteria for assessments of PTSD as outlined in DSM-IV (American Psychiatric Association [APA], 1994). A structured clinical interview was used to ensure coverage of all the relevant signs and symptoms of PTSD. Interview techniques were used for making diagnoses and for collecting systematic empirical data on PTSD (Watson, 1990; Weiss, 1993).

The characteristic symptoms of PTSD resulting from the exposure to extreme traumas include persistent reexperiencing of the traumatic event, persistent avoidance of stimuli associated with the trauma and numbing of general responsiveness, and persistent symptoms of increased arousal. The full symptom picture must be present for more than one month, and the disturbance must cause clinically significant distress or impairment in social, occupational, or other important areas of functioning (APA, 1994).

Psychiatric Symptom Index

The psychiatric symptom index (PSI) (Ilfeld, 1976) was used to measure the intensity of psychiatric symptomatology in terms of four syndromes: depression, anxiety, anger, and cognitive disturbance.

The PSI was translated into Arabic, and the content validity of the translated Arabic version was assessed by comparing the pairs of original and back-translated items. Overall, the back translation of each item closely reflected the symptom content of the original item. The theoretical structure of the four symptom dimensions of the PSI was subjected to a confirmatory analysis with varimax rotation. Appendix A presents the outcome of the analysis, along with the outcomes obtained by Ilfeld (1976), and indicates a degree of confirmation. Most of the loadings are higher than .40 and, for some items, even higher than those obtained in the original study. This analysis yielded four factors with eigenvalues greater than 1.0. Factor 1 contained many of the anxiety items of the original Ilfeld anxiety subscale. It also contained three items from the cognitive disturbance subscale. Factor 2 had loaded items that were in the original depression subscale, in addition to two items from the anxiety scale. Factor 3 contained all of the original items in the anger subscale. Factor 4 contained mainly items from the original depression scale that had a despair theme. The percentage of variance explained by each of these factors was as follows: 35.2 percent, 5.7 percent, 5.1 percent, and 4.2 percent, respectively. Cronbach's alpha for the total scale was .92.

Well-Being Scale

The well-being scale (WBS) is a nine-item scale measuring the psychological well-being of people in terms of a variety of emotions, physical and mental strength, and active force. The words "happy," "cheerful," and "delighted" were used to measure happiness; "relaxed," "calm," and "safe" to measure peacefulness; and "active," "responsive," and "healthy" to measure vigorousness. Participants were asked to report to what extent they felt each emotion and state during the past month. The ratings were made on a four-point scale (0 = not at all; 4 = extremely), with the high scores indicating high well-being and the low scores indicating low well-being.

Using a principal-component analysis with a varimax rotation of eigenvalues greater than or equal to 1.0, the scale generated two factors. Only items with loadings of at least .50 were selected to be included among the factors. These factors with their loadings are listed in Appendix B. Factor 1, happiness and peacefulness, explained 47.7 percent of the variance. Factor 2, vigorousness, explained 13.6 percent of the variance. Cronbach's alpha for the total scale was .86.

Trauma-Induced Stress Scale

The trauma-induced stress scale (TISS) is an eleven-item scale measuring the capacity of the traumatic event to induce stress within the various dimensions of an individual's life. What constitutes stress, as conceptualized in this scale, was determined partly by the stimulus-oriented theories (Elliot and Eisdorfer, 1982) that focus measurement on the characteristics of the individual's environment (e.g., external and internal noxious conditions) that will accurately reflect cumulative stress.

Using a principal-component analysis with a varimax rotation of eigenvalues greater than or equal to 1.0, the scale generated three factors: (1) strains in work and family, (2) strains in family relationships, and (3) strains in marriage and health. Only items with loadings of at least .50 were selected to be included among the factors. Appendix C presents factor loadings and the TISS items on their respective factors. Cronbach's alpha for the TISS was .82.

Role Strains Scale

The role strains scale (RSS) was developed to measure role strain, role conflict, role overload, and role functioning experienced by people within various life domains.

The initial selection of items was guided, in part, by early theoretical formulations of role strain (Goode, 1960; Merton, 1968), and by those role strains appearing on other role strain inventories (e.g., Pearlin and Schooler, 1978).

A factor analysis of nineteen items, using a principal-component analysis with a varimax rotation of eigenvalues greater than or equal to 1.0 resulted in the formation of five factors. These five factors with their loadings are listed in Appendix D. Factor 1 reflected increased role demands regarding family finances and supply, parenting, and family member care. Factor 2 represented increased role strains in regard to the absence of a spouse, dependency needs arising from injury or illness of a family member, and disagreement with collateral relatives. Factor 3 focused on interrole conflict that reflected outdoor and indoor work. Factor 4 measured increased role strains in regard to role obligations such as parenting, homemaking, and helping children with schoolwork. Factor 5, a single item, represented increased role strain in satisfying spousal needs. Cronbach's alpha for the total scale was .82.

Ideology Scale

The ideology scale (IS) was designed to assess individuals' generalized attitudes and commitments to their political party and religion.

A factor analysis of eleven items using a principal-component analysis with a varimax rotation of eigenvalues greater than or equal to 1.0 resulted in the formation of three factors associated with (1) attitudes toward political party, (2) commitment to religion as faith and practice (e.g., laws and legislation), and (3) commitment to politicoreligious principles and practices. These factors and their loadings are listed in Appendix E. Cronbach's alpha for the total scale was .75.

Social Support Scale

The social support scale (SSS) was designed to measure the respondents' perceived social support from immediate family members (i.e., nuclear family), collateral relatives (i.e., extended family), friends, and community support (e.g., religious groups, political parties, charitable organizations, and professional services networks). Functions of social support reflected emotional support, advice, encouragement, financial aid, companionship, and boosting morale.

The items of the scale were declarative statements to which the respondent answered "agree" (2), "disagree" (1), or "don't know" (not scored).

A factor analysis of twenty-five items, using a principal-component analysis with a varimax rotation of eigenvalues greater than or equal to 1.0, generated four factors. Only factor loadings of .50 were selected to represent factors. These factors with their loadings are listed in Appendix F. Factor 1 reflected support received from significant others. Four distinct resources were represented, namely, support received from linear relatives (i.e., companionship, emotional and financial support, encouragement, advice); from collateral relatives (intimacy, encouragement); from friends (companionship, attentiveness); and support received from professional helpers. Factor 2 represented the provision and receipt of social support from social institutions (professional and financial). Factor 3 focused on religious group support (moral, financial, problem solving). Factor 4 included support from political groups (moral, financial). Cronbach's alpha for the total scale is .91.

Coping Scale

The coping scale (CS) was designed to measure coping styles and strategies utilized by a person in difficult or problematic situations.

Coping responses, as conceptualized in this scale, have been guided by earlier coping assessment procedures (e.g., Billings and Moos, 1981). Factor analytic procedures, using a principal-component analysis with a varimax rotation of eigenvalues greater than or equal to 1.0, resulted in the formation of five factors. These factors and their loadings are listed in Appendix G. Factor 1 reflected problem-focused coping responses. Strategies included seeking information, advice, and help from significant others (e.g., friends and relatives) and from the professional services networks (e.g., clergymen and physicians), as well as seeking spiritual support (e.g., praying and engaging in religious activities). Factor 2 represented emotion-focused coping such as emotional discharge (e.g., crying and expressing anger), resigned acceptance (e.g., accepting a situation and restructuring it to find something favorable), and effort to receive social support from significant others (e.g., family and other relatives). Factor 3 centered around seeking support from significant others such as the family (information, advice, moral and financial support). Factor 4 measured seeking support from political and religious groups (information, advice, help). Factor 5 reflected autonomy and independence in dealing with problematic situations (problem solving, decision making). Cronbach's alpha for the total scale was .91.

Sociopolitical Satisfaction Scale

The sociopolitical satisfaction scale (SPSS) was designed to assess an individual's degree of satisfaction with the various sociopolitical life domains. The evaluations of items were rated on a seven-point rating scale ranging from 1 (very dissatisfied) to 7 (very satisfied) so that scores ranged from 13 (lowest satisfaction) to 91 (highest possible satisfaction).

Using a principal-component analysis with a varimax rotation of eigenvalues greater than or equal to 1.0, three factors were generated. Only items that had factor loadings of at least .50

were selected to represent factors. These factors and their loadings are listed in Appendix H. Factor 1 reflected the degree of satisfaction with the political situation in terms of achievement, safety, and peace. Factor 2 represented the degree of satisfaction with work as reflected in wages and benefits, future security, personal growth, and feelings of worth. Factor 3 focused on the degree of satisfaction with social life in terms of zest for life, social relationships, and social security. Cronbach's alpha for the total scale was .80.

Statistical Analysis

Logistic regression was used to predict perceived psychological distress as reflected by post-traumatic stress disorder (PTSD), psychiatric symptomatology, and psychological well-being. Inclusion of many of the demographics and contextual variables is important since they are viewed as factors that influence the adaptation to traumatic events.

Logistic regression does not require strict assumptions about multivariate normal distributions. It has been developed to analyze the probability of relatively rare binomial-distributed events (Hosmer and Lemeshow, 1989). As a result, this method requires fewer assumptions and is statistically more robust than other procedures, such as multiple regression or discriminant function analysis. This makes it suitable for analyzing relatively low prevalence outcomes such as PTSD. All logistic regressions presented are "simultaneous models," which means that all variables are adjusted (i.e., controlled) for all other variables in the model simultaneously. For each regression, odds ratio (OR), r, and R^2 statistics are provided. The r and R^2 statistics in logistic regression are useful analogs to the partial r correlation and the R^2 statistics in linear regression, respectively, but are not fully equivalent (see Hosmer and Lemeshow, 1989; Kleinbaum, Kupper, and Morgenstern, 1982). To denote this, the subscript "p" is used (i.e., r_p and R^2_p) to indicate that these should be interpreted as "pseudo" r and R^2 statistics, respectively. In cases in which the predictor variable is significant and is a dichotomous variable (e.g., type of trauma), the OR is reported in the text and is readily interpretable: it indicates the odds of having a current disorder when the predictor variable changes from 0 to 1, controlling for all other variables in the model. When the predictor has more than two categories (e.g., social support), the OR represents the change in the odds of having a current disorder per unit change in the predictor variable and, hence, is not as readily interpretable in terms of effect magnitude. Consequently, when a predictor is significant and has more than two categories, the "r" analog ("r_p") is reported in the text instead of the OR.

Multivariate analysis of variance (MANOVA), t-tests, and chi-square analyses were employed to examine the difference in perceived psychiatric symptomatology (i.e., PSI) and PTSD, as a function of type of trauma, and demographics. All statistical analyses were performed using SPSS-PC+[tm] Version 5.0 (Norusis, 1992).

PART II: QUALITATIVE STUDY

Sample Selection

Participants were recruited through two agencies that worked with affected people during the *intifada:* Young Men's Christian Association (YMCA) and the Ex-detainees Rehabilitation Program. They were randomly selected through the existing database of affected family members categorized by sociodemographic features and characterized by homogeneity, but with sufficient variation among participants to allow for contrasting opinions (Knodel, 1993; Krueger, 1994). Homogeneity was sought in gender, age, and educational level. The number of participants in each group was eight, which is considered moderate (Morgan, 1988). This size ensured the contribution of each individual and facilitated managing the discussions.

To recruit family members, payment of New Israeli Sheqels (NIS) 100 was given to each person for each session. The monetary incentives served as a stimulus to attend the sessions (Morgan, 1988), since participation incurred expenses of travel, time, effort, and loss of a day's wages for those who were employed. The participants showed great interest in the issues that were discussed because they touched the reality of their lives. They were acquainted with the aims of the study, the possible uses of the information, and the manner in which they could aid in the research. Confidentiality was safeguarded, and the right of the men and women to abstain from or terminate participation at any time was secured. This right helped them feel safe and not at risk by participating in the study.

Participants

A total of sixty-four family members who were affected by political violence during the *intifada* agreed to participate in the group discussions; of these, twenty-three (35.9 percent) had a family member imprisoned, seventeen (26.6 percent) one who was killed, fourteen (21.9 percent) one who was injured and sustained a disability, and ten (15.6 percent) had a house demolished. They came from various geographic regions of the West Bank and the Gaza Strip and represented refugee camps, and urban and rural areas. The participants, one-half of whom were women, were predominantly Muslims, 87.5 percent; 12.5 percent were Christians; 82.8 percent were currently married, and the remaining were widowed. They ranged in age from thirty to sixty-five years ($M = 48.6$, $SD = 12.8$). Of the participants, 76 percent had a preparatory school education or less, while 24 percent had secondary education or some college. Approximately 87.5 percent of the women were housewives, 9.4 percent were teachers, and one was a nurse. Of the men, 70 percent were laborers, 23.3 percent unemployed, and

6.7 percent were teachers. The combined monthly income of the participants' families ranged from 50 to 650 U.S. dollars ($M = 275$).

Moderators

The groups were guided by four skillful moderators in a variety of locations: the YMCA, Ex-detainees Rehabilitation Program, and the Palestinian Academic Society for the Study of International Affairs. The groups of female participants were conducted by a female moderator team of a moderator and an assistant moderator, whereas male groups were conducted by a male moderator team. The moderators had postgraduate degrees in psychology, social work, or sociology; were familiar with group processes; had previous experience in working with groups; and had been trained in group dynamics. Moderators were also trained by the researcher to adopt roles that ease entry, facilitate receptivity of participants, and elicit cooperation, trust, openness, and acceptance. They demonstrated that they could control the topics that were discussed and the dynamics of the group in such a way that the people involved were not threatened. Moderators were guided to obtain the most useful information from participants while attempting to keep their comments in regard to sensitive issues as nondirective as possible. However, the level of moderator involvement was high when they judged that unproductive discussion should be cut off, and when they probed to produce what the research objectives intended to elicit. The moderators in the study were interacting as Palestinians with Palestinians, exploring, but doing so with an interest in the welfare of the participant families.

The moderators in the study were primarily concerned with directing the discussion, keeping the conversation flowing, but taking few notes. The assistants, however, took comprehensive notes, operated tape recorders, and handled the environmental conditions and logistics (refreshments, seating, etc.).

Focus Group Discussions

The moderators knew in advance which specific aspects of the traumatic experience they would have the respondents cover in their discussion (Denzin, 1970; Morgan, 1988; Seltiz et al., 1965). A guide was prepared by the researcher to enable the moderators to organize the discussion topics in more or less the same order from group to group (Wells, 1974). In developing the guide, the questioning route was preferred because there were different moderators (Krueger, 1994). This format could achieve the exact content desired and ensure that each question was exactly what the research aims intended.

Although the guide helped in channeling the group interaction, the moderators had considerable latitude within the framework of the guide and could redefine the order of questioning to fit the characteristics of the conversation (Denzin, 1970; Wells, 1974). This feature of the focused discussion was based on the assumption that the most effective sequence for any respondent is determined by his or her readiness and willingness to take up a topic as it arises (Denzin, 1970; Richardson, Dohrenwend, and Klein, 1965). Allowing respondents this freedom resulted in the raising of important issues not contained in the guide. Appendix I presents the guide for focus group discussions.

Coding System

Audiotapes of the group discussions were transcribed verbatim. The researcher identified the common, salient themes that appeared consistently in the transcripts.

A coding manual was created consisting of detailed descriptions of the ten themes. The manual was used to train two coders who worked independently and read through the eight transcripts. In the transcripts, 829 codable passages had been marked, and the coders identified the theme that they judged best described the marked passage. Reliability of the coding system was assessed by measuring the agreement between the ratings of the researcher and each independent coder. Cohen's kappa, a measure of percentage agreement that removes the effect of chance agreement, was .95 between the author and rater No. 1 and .88 between the author and rater No. 2; and the percentage agreement for the ten themes ranged from 100 to 81 percent.

Chapter 3

Trauma, Mental Health, and Mediators

Mental health researchers have made enormous strides in documenting the many links between traumatic events, mediating factors, and important psychological outcomes such as post-traumatic stress disorder, psychiatric disorders, and psychological well-being. These efforts have contributed to a better understanding of the multidimensional nature of the posttrauma environment and to the central role it plays in determining victims' reactions. Despite these impressive developments, several sociopolitical factors still need to be addressed, such as ideology and satisfaction with the sociopolitical situation. Also, little attention has been paid to the multifaceted nature of political traumas and to the ongoing disruptive stressors associated with the traumatic events. This chapter examines some of these topics and seeks to offer a social-ecological perspective from which to examine them.

The chapter consists of four sections. First, empirical findings on the predictors of PTSD, psychiatric symptomatology, and psychological well-being are presented. A number of variables are included: type of trauma, trauma-induced stress and role strains, family members' characteristics and sociodemographics, and psychosocial mediators such as support resources, coping behavior, ideology, and level of satisfaction with the sociopolitical situation. The next two sections indicate the prevalence of PTSD and psychiatric symptomatology across type of political trauma, socioeconomic status, personal characteristics, geographical re-

gions, and residential patterns, followed by findings on mediators contributing to positive outcomes under high-stress and low-
stress conditions. The chapter concludes with a discussion of the
results in light of the existing scientific literature.

MENTAL HEALTH STATUS

The results of the logistic regressions are shown in Table 3.1.
They indicate that PTSD was positively associated with families
with one member who was killed, with families from the Gaza
Strip, with gender, and with trauma-induced stress. It was negatively associated with families with one member who was imprisoned.
The odds ratio for type of trauma was significant (OR = 2.07,
$p < .01$), indicating that for families of a killed member the chances
(odds) of having a current PTSD diagnosis, controlling for other
variables in this model, were about 2.07 times higher than for other
types of trauma. However, families with various types of trauma
(OR = .42; $p < .0008$) were more likely to receive a PTSD diagnosis than families of the imprisoned. In addition, families from the
Gaza Strip (OR = 3.65, $p < .001$), women (OR = 2.21, $p < .0001$),
and those with higher levels of trauma-induced stress (r_p = .12;
$p < .0001$) were more likely to receive a PTSD diagnosis, controlling for the other variables, including type of trauma.

As with PTSD, after controlling for other variables, trauma-
induced stress was still a significant predictor of psychiatric symptoms (r_p = .29; $p < .00001$), although now it was increased substantially (r_p = .12 versus r_p = .29). Other important predictors of
psychiatric symptomatology were role strains (r_p = .05; $p < .01$).
Psychiatric disorders were negatively associated with employment
status (OR = .67; $p < .03$), education (r_p = $-.04$; $p < .04$), and
social support (r_p = $-.04$; $p < .02$), indicating that those who were
unemployed, those who had less education, and those with lower
social support were more likely to develop psychiatric disorders
(see Table 3.1).

TABLE 3.1. Multiple Logistic Regressions Predicting PTSD, Psychiatric Symptoms, and Well-Being

Variables	PTSD			Psychiatric Symptomatology			Well-Being		
	b	r_p	OR	b	r_p	OR	b	r_p	OR
Killed	.73	.06	2.07**	−.38	.00	.67	.21	.00	1.24
Houses demolished	−.19	.00	.82	−.25	.00	.77	−.22	.00	.79
Imprisoned	−.86	−.09	.42****	.14	.00	1.16	−.47	.04	.62*
Injured	−.06	.00	.93	−.44	−.01	.64	−.33	.00	.71
Gender	.79	.12	2.21****	.29	.02	1.34	.05	.00	1.06
Age	.01	.03	1.01	−.00	.00	.99	.02	.05	1.02*
Income	1.59	.00	1.00	2.37	.00	1.00	−6.6	.00	1.00
Education	.00	.00	1.00	−.04	−.04	.95*	−.00	.00	.99
West Bank	.40	.00	1.49	−.14	.00	.86	1.56	.10	4.79****
Gaza Strip	1.29	.08	3.65***	−.36	.00	.69	.44	.00	1.55
Married	−.37	−.01	.68	−.27	.00	.75	−.51	−.03	.59

39

TABLE 3.1 (continued)

Variables	PTSD			Psychiatric Symptomatology			Well-Being		
	b	r_p	OR	b	r_p	OR	b	r_p	OR
Employed	−.11	.00	.88	−.39	−.04	.67*	−.10	.00	.89
Traumatic stress	.04	.12	1.04****	.11	.28	1.12****	−.00	.00	.99
Role strains	−.00	.00	.99	.02	.05	1.02**	.00	.00	1.00
Coping	−.01	.00	.98	.00	.00	1.00	−.01	.00	.98
Social support	.01	.00	1.01	−.03	−.04	.96*	−.00	.00	.99
Sociopolitical satisfaction	.00	.00	1.00	−.00	.00	.99	−.07	−.26	.92***
Ideology	−.01	.00	.89	−.00	.00	.99	−.01	.00	.98
Constant	−2.62*			−2.80*			2.53*		
Model x^2	116.30****			226.31****			246.72****		

Types of Trauma are coded: Other Types of Trauma (ott) = 0; Killed = 1. ott = 0; Houses Demolished = 1. ott = 0; Imprisoned = 1. ott = 0; Injured = 1. Gender is coded: Male = 0; Female = 1. Age is coded: Age in Years. Income is coded: Family Monthly Income in U.S. Dollars. Education is coded: Number of Years in Education. West Bank is coded: Other = 0; West Bank = 1. Gaza Strip is coded: Other = 0; Gaza Strip = 1. Married is coded: Not Married = 0; Married = 1. Employment is coded: Currently unemployed = 0; Currently employed = 1. Traumatic Stress is coded: 5-point scale ranging from 11 to 55. Role Strains is coded: 5-point scale ranging from 19 to 95. Social Support is coded: 2-point scale ranging from 25 to 50. Coping is coded: 2-point scale ranging from 33 to 66. Sociopolitical Satisfaction is coded: 7-point scale ranging from 13 to 91. Ideology is coded: 5-point scale ranging from 11 to 55.

* p < .05
** p < .001
*** p < .001
**** p < .0001

The regression for well-being, as shown in Table 3.1, indicated that well-being was positively associated with families from the West Bank and with age; it was negatively associated with families of the imprisoned and with sociopolitical satisfaction.

The odds ratio for families from different geographical regions was substantial for this logistic regression (OR = 4.79; p < .0001), indicating that for West Bankers, the chances of having lower well-being, controlling for other variables in this model, were about 4.7 times higher than for families from Jerusalem and the Gaza Strip.

Age was positively associated with well-being (r_p = .05; p < .02), indicating lower well-being for older people. Families with multiple traumas (OR = .62; p < .03) were more likely to have lower psychological well-being than families of those who were imprisoned. In addition, those with lower levels of sociopolitical satisfaction (r_p = − .26; p <. 00001) were more likely to have lower psychological well-being.

POST-TRAUMATIC STRESS DISORDER

Judged on the basis of the DSM-IV diagnostic criteria for PTSD, 315 persons (35 percent) in the sample met full criteria for PTSD diagnosis after they had been exposed to traumatic political events. Only two cases had a delayed onset; that is, the onset of symptoms occurred more than six months after the trauma.

The rate of PTSD varied significantly across types of events (x^2 = 26.47, df = 4, p = 0.0001). Experiencing a family member killed had a higher rate (49.3 percent) than having a family member imprisoned (17.6 percent), a house demolished (28.1 percent), a family member injured (32.9 percent), or undergoing more than one traumatic event (37.9 percent).

The prevalence of PTSD was higher in women than men, 44.6 percent against 26.1 percent, an expected difference given women's known greater likelihood to develop PTSD after experiencing traumatic events. Among those who met full criteria for PTSD diagnosis, 61.3 percent of women had PTSD compared with 38.7 percent of men. The prevalence of PTSD was unrelated to respondents' age or religion.

In regard to socioeconomic variables, the rate of PTSD was associated with income ($x^2 = 15.66$, $df = 3$, $p < .001$), but not with education. However, the highest and lowest income levels had the highest rates of PTSD (40.8 percent and 38.6 percent) compared to those with moderate income levels (32.9 percent and 16.9 percent).

With respect to roles and status, significant differences were found between PTSD status and marital status ($x^2 = 16.05$, $df = 3$, $p < .001$). The widowed (53.2 percent) and the divorced (54.5 percent) had the highest rates of PTSD compared to the married (33.3 percent) and those who were married more than once (23.3 percent).

Significant differences were found between PTSD status and occupation ($x^2 = 26.9$, $df = 5$, $p < .0001$). Homemakers (44.4 percent) and the unemployed (34.2 percent) had the highest rates of PTSD compared to teachers (29.8 percent), laborers (26.6 percent), service, technical, and sales occupations (26 percent), and agricultural workers (20.5 percent).

In regard to cultural variables, the rate of PTSD was associated with geographic location ($x^2 = 24.11$, $df = 2$, $p < .0001$) but was unrelated to residential patterns (i.e., city, village, camp) or to refugee and nonrefugee status. Jerusalemites (20 percent) had a lower rate than residents of the West Bank (31.3 percent). A markedly higher rate (47 percent) was observed in Gaza Strip residents.

PTSD and Role Strains

Characteristics of family members were examined in more detail by dividing participants into four groups using median splits for high/low role strains (based on the role strains measure) and PTSD/non-PTSD symptomatology (based on the DSM-IV): high role strain/PTSD (n = 148), high role strain/non-PTSD (n = 279), low role strain/PTSD (n = 167), low role strain/non-PTSD (n = 306). These groups were then contrasted using a series of one-way MANOVAs, multivariate analyses of variance. This analytic format was selected over a 2 × 2 MANOVA because of the primary interest in cell comparisons rather than main effects or interactions addressed by omnibus MANOVAs.

Multivariate analysis of variance was performed to investigate the effect of these four groups on sociopolitical satisfaction, ideology, social support, and coping. The results indicated that the groups are significantly different (Hotellings' T = .09, approximate F = 7.02, p < .0001). Univariate F tests indicated that both groups with low levels of role strains had significantly higher levels of sociopolitical satisfaction ($F(3,894)$ = 22.56, p < .0001) regardless of their PTSD status. In addition, the low-role-strain/ PTSD group had significantly higher levels of social support ($F(3,895)$ = 3.39, p < .01) than the high-role-strain/PTSD group, indicating that among those who had a PTSD diagnosis, those with higher social support were more likely to report lower levels of role strain. There were no significant differences for ideology or coping (see Table 3.2).

Given the significant group differences obtained for both the sociopolitical satisfaction and social support domains, two additional multivariate tests were conducted to investigate which of the sociopolitical satisfaction and social support subscales accounted for the difference. MANOVA results yielded significant main effects of the groups on sociopolitical satisfaction (T = .09, F = 9.27, p <. 0001). The group effect was due to higher levels of satisfaction with the political situation ($F(3,895)$ = 19.73, p < .0001), satisfaction with work ($F(3,894)$ = 5.69, p < .0007), and satisfaction with social life ($F(3,895)$ = 10.56, p < .0001) in both the low-role-strain groups.

TABLE 3.2. Comparisons of Role Strains and PTSD Subsets on Sociopolitical Satisfaction and Social Support Variables

Variables	High Role Strain/ PTSD M	High Role Strain/ Non-PTSD M	Low Role Strain/ PTSD M	Low Role Strain/ Non-PTSD M
Sociopolitical satisfaction scale	36.33	36.37	43.87	41.87
Satisfaction with political situation	11.68	11.81	16.11	13.94
Satisfaction with work	15.69	15.55	17.23	17.32
Satisfaction with social life	8.95	9.30	10.51	10.63
Social support scale	31.69	32.77	34.04	33.01
Support from significant others	18.94	19.61	20.34	19.74
Support from institutions	6.01	6.35	6.71	6.33

MANOVA results yielded significant main effects for group on social support (T = .02, F = 1.90, p < .02). Univariate F tests indicated significant main effects for group on support from significant others ($F(3,895)$ = 3.27, p < .02) and support from institutions ($F(3,895)$ = 3.26, p < .02). Scheffé test results indicated that the low-role-strain/PTSD group received more support from significant others and from institutions than did the high-role-strain/PTSD group (see Table 3.2).

PTSD and Trauma-Induced Stress

Subjects were divided into four groups using median splits for high/low trauma-induced stress (based on the trauma-induced stress scale) and PTSD/non-PTSD symptomatology: high traumatic stress/PTSD (n = 174), high traumatic stress/non-PTSD (n = 257), low traumatic stress/PTSD (n = 141), and low traumatic stress/non-PTSD (n = 328). MANOVA results indicated no significant differences among the groups on sociopolitical satisfaction, ideology, coping, and social support.

PSYCHIATRIC SYMPTOMATOLOGY

Multivariate analysis of variance was used to determine whether any differences in psychiatric symptomatology existed among family members with various types of traumas. The MANOVA results revealed significant main effects for type of traumas on depression ($F(4,895)$ = 4.58, p < .001) and on anxiety and despair ($F(4,895)$ = 2.54, p < .03). However, when the Scheffé test was used, families with multiple types of traumas demonstrated a higher level of depression (M = 49.03) than did families of those who were injured (M = 40.05), whereas families with various types of traumas showed no significant differences on anxiety and despair.

In regard to individual dispositional variables, the results indicated significant main effects for gender (T = .06, F = 12.06,

$p < .0001$). Table 3.3 shows the results of uncorrelated t-tests indicating that women demonstrated a higher level of anxiety and despair (t (898) = $-5.14, p < .01$) than did men.

To evaluate the effect of age on psychiatric symptomatology, three age categories were identified: those who were under thirty-four years of age, those from thirty-five to forty-five, and those forty-six and older. MANOVA results indicated significant main effects for age ($T = .02, F = 2.97, p < .003$). Univariate F tests revealed significant differences on anxiety and cognitive disturbance ($F(2,897) = 8.44, p < .0002)$ and on depression ($F (2,897) = 4.86, p < .007$). A post hoc Scheffé test indicated that the oldest group reported higher levels of anxiety and cognitive disturbance and depression than did the two younger groups (see Table 3.3).

A two-way (education × income) MANOVA was also conducted on the psychiatric symptom index. No significant interaction was found. Education and income independently influenced respondents' psychiatric symptomatology. There were main effects for education ($T = .07, F = 3.96, p < .0001$) and income ($T = .05, F = 4.25, p < .0001$).

Univariate F tests indicated significant differences on anxiety and cognitive disturbance ($F(4,895) = 18.73, p < .0001$), depression ($F(4,895) = 15.33, p < .0001$), and anxiety and despair ($F(4,880) = 3.37, p < .0001$), with illiterates having higher scores than those who had some education or higher education. There were no significant effects for anger. Significant main effects were found for income on anxiety and cognitive disturbances ($F(3,896) = 7.80, p < .0001$) on anxiety and despair ($F(3,896) = 6.20, p < .0004$), with those having low monthly incomes scoring higher than the other income level groups. No significant differences were found for income on depression or anger subscales (see Table 3.3).

A two-way (marital status × employment status) MANOVA was conducted on the psychiatric symptom index. Significant

TABLE 3.3. Means of Psychiatric Symptom Index and Demographics

Demographics	Anxiety and Cognitive Disturbance	Depression	Anger	Anxiety and Despair
Gender				
Male (n = 467)	-----	-----	-----	30.52
Female (n = 433)	-----	-----	-----	38.35
Age				
Under 35 years (n = 178)	34.06	43.70	-----	-----
36 to 45 years (n = 197)	33.54	44.49	-----	-----
46 years and older (n = 525)	40.26	49.17	-----	-----
Education				
Illiterate (n = 192)	49.39	58.00	-----	40.19
Elementary (n = 233)	37.41	47.33	-----	32.54
Preparatory (n = 175)	30.43	43.64	-----	32.28
Secondary (n = 185)	34.57	42.70	-----	33.66
Higher education (n = 115)	30.43	40.64	-----	32.02
Income (US$), monthly				
Less than 300 (n = 376)	41.48	-----	-----	38.05
301 to 600 (n = 322)	33.17	-----	-----	31.41
601 to 900 (n = 77)	34.74	-----	-----	29.43
901 and above (n = 125)	38.76	-----	-----	33.37
Employment status				
Employed (n = 359)	32.56	-----	-----	-----
Unemployed (n = 541)	40.87	-----	-----	-----
Geographical region				
West Bank (n = 598)	-----	-----	41.47	-----
Gaza Strip (n = 249)	-----	-----	34.10	-----
Jerusalem (n = 53)	-----	-----	28.14	-----

Note: Only means with $p < .05$ are presented in the table.

47

multivariate effects were not obtained for the interaction. However, there was a significant multivariate effect for marital status ($T = .02$, $F = 5.75$, $p < .0001$) and employment status ($T = .01$, $F = 2.94$, $p < .0001$). Univariate t-tests indicated that no significant differences existed between the unmarried and married, whereas the umemployed demonstrated higher levels of anxiety and cognitive disturbance ($T(898) = -5.37$, $p < .01$) than did the employed (see Table 3.3).

In analyzing cultural variables, a two-way MANOVA (geographic region × residential patterns) was conducted on the psychiatric symptom index. Significant multivariate effects were obtained for the interaction ($T = .04$, $F = 2.64$, $p < .0001$). A significant interaction effect was found for anxiety and cognitive disturbance ($F(4,891) = 3.02$, $p < .01$) and for anxiety and despair ($F(4,891) = 2.43$, $p < .04$). Significant multivariate effects were also obtained for residential patterns ($T = .02$, $F = 2.67$, $p < .006$). Univariate F tests revealed significant differences on anxiety and cognitive disturbance ($F(2,891) = 3.59$, $p < .02$). However, when a Scheffé test was used, no significant differences were found among families from urban areas, rural areas, or refugee camps.

MANOVA results revealed a significant overall effect for geographic location ($T = .05$, $F = 6.15$, $p < .0001$). Univariate F tests indicated significant differences on depression ($F(2,897) = 3.31$, $p < .03$) and anger ($F(2,897) = 12.03$, $p < .0001$). Post hoc Scheffé analysis indicated that West Bank residents reported more anger than Jerusalemites and Gazans, whereas there were no significant differences among the groups on depression (see Table 3.3).

Psychiatric Symptomatology and Role Strains

The sample was divided into four groups using median splits for high/low role strains and high/low psychiatric symptomatology (based on the psychiatric symptom index): high role strain/

high psychiatric symptoms (n = 247), high role strain/low psychiatric symptoms (n = 180), low role strain/high psychiatric symptoms (n = 212), and low role strain/low psychiatric symptoms (n = 261).

Multivariate analysis of variance was performed to investigate the effects of the four groups on sociopolitical satisfaction, ideology, social support, and coping. The results indicated that the groups are significantly different (T = .12, F = 9.60, p < .0001).

Univariate F tests revealed significant main group effects on sociopolitical satisfaction ($F(3,894)$ = 26.34, p < .0001). Scheffé test results indicated that low role strain/low psychiatric symptomatology had higher levels of sociopolitical satisfaction than all other groups. The low role strain/high psychiatric symptomatology group had higher scores than the two high-role-strain groups (see Table 3.4).

F tests also revealed significant main group effects on social support ($F(3,895)$ = 6.87, p < .0001), with the low role strain/low psychiatric symptomatology having higher scores than did the high role strain/high psychiatric symptomatology and low role strain/high psychiatric symptomatology (see Table 3.4).

Further analysis indicated significant main effects on satisfaction with the political situation ($F(3,895)$ = 16.81, p < .0001) and satisfaction with work ($F(3,895)$ = 10.81, p < .0001), with the low-role-strain groups having higher scores than did the high-role-strain groups. Results also showed significant main group effects on satisfaction with life ($F(3,895)$ = 13.67, p < .0001), with the low-role-strain/low-psychiatric-symptomatology group having higher scores than did all the other groups (see Table 3. 4).

Significant main group effects on receiving support from significant others were revealed ($F(3,895)$ = 3.16, p < .02). However, when the Scheffé test was used, no significant differences in groups were seen. Significant main group effects on support from religious groups ($F(3,895)$ = 9.71, p < .0001) and support from political faction ($F(3,895)$ = 7.89, p <. 0001), with both the

TABLE 3.4. Mean Comparisons of Role Strains and Psychiatric Disorders Subsets on Sociopolitical Satisfaction and Social Support Variables

Variables	High Role Strain/ High Psychiatric Disorders M	High Role Strain/ Low Psychiatric Disorders M	Low Role Strain/ High Psychiatric Disorders M	Low Role Strain/ Low Psychiatric Disorders M
Sociopolitical satisfaction	37.57	35.15	40.84	43.97
Satisfaction with political situation	11.86	11.63	14.06	15.23
Satisfaction with work	16.51	14.36	16.84	17.65
Satisfaction with social life	9.20	9.15	9.98	11.09
Social support	31.66	33.41	32.41	34.14
Support from religious groups	3.30	4.40	3.60	4.13
Support from political party	2.70	3.43	2.78	3.27

low-psychiatric-symptomatology groups having higher scores than did both the high-psychiatric-symptomatology groups (see Table 3.4).

Psychiatric Symptomatology and Traumatic Stress

Subjects were divided into four groups using median splits for high/low trauma-induced stress and high/low psychiatric symptomatology: high traumatic stress/high psychiatric symptomatology (n = 309), high traumatic stress/low psychiatric symptomatology (n = 122), low traumatic stress/high psychiatric symptomatology (n = 151), and low traumatic stress/low psychiatric symptomatology (n = 318). MANOVA was performed to investigate the effect of the four groups on sociopolitical satisfaction, ideology, social support, and coping. The results indicated that the groups are significantly different (T = .04, F = 3.37, p < .0001). Univariate F tests indicated that there were significant main group effects on social support (F (3,896) = 6.87, p < .0001), with both the low-psychiatric-symptomatology groups having higher scores than did the high-psychiatric-symptomatology groups (see Table 3.5). There were no significant differences on sociopolitical satisfaction, ideology, or coping.

For further analysis of social support, MANOVA results yielded significant main group effects on support from religious groups ($F(3,896)$ = 11.15, p < .0001) and support from political party ($F(3,896)$ = 7.51, p < .0001), with both the low-psychiatric-symptomatology having higher scores than did the high-psychiatric-symptomatology groups (see Table 3.5).

DISCUSSION

The level of post-traumatic stress disorder (PTSD) found in Palestinian family members who experienced *intifada*-related trauma, 35 percent, was markedly high. An affected person who

TABLE 3.5. Mean Comparisons of Traumatic Stress and Psychiatric Disorders Subsets on Social Support Variables

Variables	High Traumatic Stress/High Psychiatric Disorders M	High Traumatic Stress/Low Psychiatric Disorders M	Low Traumatic Stress/High Psychiatric Disorders M	Low Traumatic Stress/Low Psychiatric Disorders M
Overall social support	31.84	34.60	32.41	33.55
Support from religious groups	3.28	4.56	3.76	4.11
Support from political party	2.69	3.31	2.77	3.41

has had a family member killed, injured, or imprisoned and a house demolished is likely to be alert for symptoms of PTSD. By definition, a wide variety of traumatic events may evoke symptoms of PTSD (Smith and North, 1993). However, results from the present study indicate that having a family member killed is a consistently significant predictor of the development of PTSD for family members, not only when examined alone, but also when examined in combination with various types of political traumas, many of which have been popularly viewed as having considerable predictive strength in the long term, such as sustaining the greatest property damage or loss of home (Lima et al., 1989; McFarlane, 1986; Parkes, 1977). In this study, people who had a family member imprisoned were noted to have better well-being than comparable family members with other types of traumas (e.g., injury, death). This may imply a response effect related to the conceptualization of the traumatic events (Green, 1993). Conceptualizations of trauma, or of what constitutes a "political trauma" in the Palestinian context, are reflected in people saying in regard to significant others (e.g., husband, son, brother), "Better imprisoned than killed, and better deported than imprisoned." This may suggest that the Palestinian definition of a trauma may vary according to the perceived magnitude and nature of the event.

An important variable that has been identified in this study as a predictor of PTSD and psychiatric symptomatology is trauma-induced stress. Naturally, most traumatic events have secondary stressors; sometimes these stressors become the main cause of new morbidity (Veltro et al., 1990; Weisaeth, 1993). These induced stressors were observed in family members' relationships, marriages, health, and work. On the other hand, role strains have contributed to family members' psychiatric symptomatology, but not to the development of PTSD. The results, therefore, imply that PTSD is particularly likely to follow stressors and strains that would be markedly associated with the traumatic event per se, and not with the normative role strains of the affected family members.

Consistent with previous studies, certain individual characteristics have been associated with psychiatric symptoms, particularly the female gender (Fairley, 1984; Gleser, Green, and Winget, 1981; Lopez-Ibor, Canas, and Rodriguez-Gamazo, 1985; Parkes, 1977). Many researchers have indicated that gender is a characteristic that influences the stressors to which people are exposed (Billings and Moos, 1984; Pearlin, 1989; Pearlin and Lieberman, 1979), as well as the personal and social mediating resources that can be utilized to deal with hardship. Also, previous research on Palestinian women (Khamis, 1998) indicated that cumulative life changes had a major impact on the psychological well-being of traumatized women. However, in a society marked by strictly defined sex roles, the behavior of women is extremely constrained, and, therefore, the overwhelming responsibilities that are placed on Palestinian women in the absence of men due to political violence (men killed, imprisoned) have been recognized as critical determinants in the development of psychological distress.

In addition, the dual nature of race and gender for Palestinian women often means exposure to stressful experiences, beginning with exploitation at work and continuing to current inequities in social resources. Perhaps the presence of the trauma engenders stress, and, as a result, women become unable to manage the hardships and difficulties of transitions and crises. Beyond the issue of number of roles per se, however, is the more intriguing question of how particular sex roles are defined, and how they may account for the negative effects of multiple-role involvement. Understanding the role of gender in psychological problems requires being aware of gender-role constructs, which may very well affect the type of psychological problems that exist, their associated symptoms, and people's response to their problems.

Stressful experiences do not arise in a vacuum but typically can be traced to surrounding social structures and people's locations within them (Pearlin, 1989). Thus, it is understandable that the results of this study indicated that the elderly had more anxiety and cognitive disturbance than the younger participants; indeed, the preponderance of studies indicates that the elderly are at highest risk (Gleser, Green, and Winget, 1981; Khamis, 1995b; Lima et al., 1987; Lopez-Ibor, Canas, and Rodriguez-Gamazo, 1985; Parkes, 1977; Shore, Tatum, and Vollmer, 1986; Wilkinson, 1983).

Consistent with previous findings (Gleser, Green, and Winget, 1981; Lopez-Ibor, Canas, and Rodriguez-Gamazo, 1985), the results indicated that lower socioeconomic level or lesser educational attainment was associated with greater symptom rates of cognitive disturbance, depression, anxiety, and despair, whereas being currently unmarried (widowed or divorced), unemployed, or a housewife was associated with PTSD (Lima et al., 1989).

Geographical region had a differential effect on family members' mental health outcomes. Gaza Strip residents had higher prevalence of PTSD, whereas West Bank residents experienced more anger and had lower well-being.

The Gaza Strip has considerably more political unrest and violence, including arbitrary arrest, beatings, raids, and torture, which may elevate rates of post-traumatic stress disorder. Gazans may be especially reluctant to divulge experiences of intensive and prolonged repression and trauma due to their vulnerable political situation. Furthermore, the Gaza Strip is a small region in which everyone knows everyone else, so that all share in the reactions of apprehension and grief of those who are exposed to political traumas. Gaza has one of the highest population densities in the world: 361 square kilometers accommodate a population of 934,000, averaging about 3,000 persons per square kilometer. To some extent, physical-geographical and sociocultural patterns govern the conditions that are perceived as particularly threatening for a population (Magnusson, 1982). In the West Bank, where the number of communities and distances between them are greater than in the Gaza Strip, services are less accessible (Nixon, 1990). It is likely that this affected responses and increased the prediction of people's anger and lower well-being.

The findings of the study document some possible long-term effects of sociopolitical satisfaction and social support. Many of the family members exposed to political traumas have high role strains and stress-related psychiatric disorders. Higher current levels of social support are associated with lower current levels of psychiatric disorders and role strains, but this does not ameliorate PTSD or the trauma-induced stress. This may suggest that the relationship with social support may not be uniform across indicators of mental health and type of stressors. This is consistent with previous findings that social support may affect those processes involved in psychosocial adjustment without appreciably reducing the arousal associated with stress (Khamis, 1993a). The types of social support seemed to vary in their impact and ability to reduce role strains when these strains were accompanied by different kinds of psychopathology. For example, it is generally agreed that social support from significant others and from institutions is associated with low role strains in people suffering from PTSD, and that social support from political and religious groups is associated with low role strains and low psychiatric disorders. Thus, there are theoretical reasons to predict the differential functional significance of types of support. This may argue for the usefulness of a specific social-support approach rather than a general social-support approach.

The results indicated further that higher levels of sociopolitical satisfaction are associated with current lower levels of psychiatric disorders and role strains, but not with PTSD and trauma-induced stress. Thus, sociopolitical satisfaction has direct positive effects on psychological well-being by fulfilling family members' needs for a stable political situation, security in work, and quality social life. By implication, the frustration of these needs may itself constitute a source of stress. With restricted alternatives, then, family members with unsatisfying conditions and/or relationships may feel powerless to alter the source of the strain, which may, in turn, be a major source of psychological distress.

Chapter 4

The Psychosocial Contexts
of Political Traumas

This chapter reflects on the content of focus group discussions, the meaning, and its particular implications. It consists of two sections. Section 1 includes descriptions of the coded themes, with verbatim examples extracted from the transcripts. The narratives depict the subjective experiences of traumatized family members regarding their posttrauma environment and recovery. The data analysis is presented in a classified form with conceptual and descriptive phrases that are generally representative of semantics in all languages. Section 2 concludes the issues in the themes according to their probable causes and effects.

SECTION I: THEMES AND NARRATIVES

Psychological and Somatic Sequelae of Trauma

Psychological responses described by participants included depression, anxiety, fear, and somatization. Men and women reported suffering from depression, experiencing feelings of sadness, dejection, and an excessive and prolonged mourning.

A man whose children were victimized said:

My son was imprisoned for three years, and one day the neighbors told me that the army was taking my son . . . so his mother went out to save him from the army . . . they burst into the house and started breaking and beating. My two-month-old daughter got burnt by the electrical heater as a result of the breaking. And they beat my children in front of my eyes . . . and when I objected they said beating them was better than killing them. My son said, "No, killing me is better than beating me." They insulted me and beat me, and my son was injured, . . . all this affected me and made me suffer. . . . I feel sad, troubled, and a wreck.

A woman experiencing multiple effects of trauma reported, "I suffer from the troubles of insomnia and instability. . . . I suffer from illness because of despair and frustration that is persistent."

The effects of the demolition of a man's house were far-reaching:

My house was demolished three times; the first time was in 1989, the second time was in 1991, and the third in 1992. This caused psychological problems for my children, who used to go to school and come back to find themselves without a house. Their mother became psychologically ill . . . . I myself went to a psychologist because of loss of appetite and physical illness that was caused by depression. Besides general feelings of sadness, despair, and frustration, certain of my thoughts and reactions were clearly related to fear.

Another man related the traumatic experiences of his sons:

My eldest son was sentenced to life in prison, and my second son was shot in the leg and was imprisoned for ten months after they beat him, causing him to be handicapped . . . he lives on medication and his health is very bad . . . he gets very frightened when he hears anybody mention the word "army." My third son gets frightened, too, but to a lesser extent . . . all this caused us physical and psychological problems.

Sleep disturbance was a common complaint, as reported by the mother of young sons:

My sons always ask, "Where is our papa?" and I always tell them that he is traveling . . . and one son always says that he has been away for a long time . . . and one son wakes up erratically during the night and asks, "Where did my papa go?" and I try to calm him down.

Others expressed milder anxiety, evoking thoughts dealing with themes such as financial concerns, along with feelings of frustration. Both were evident in this woman's statements:

Once I wanted to put some money in the bank, and my son said to me, "Don't put it in my father's name because he is always imprisoned and the money will disappear." In school he makes an effort but he is introverted and sad and he doesn't smile . . . my other children are the same because their father is in jail. . . . We wanted to visit him in jail but they told us that our request to visit him was refused. . . . I cried, and my son became sick from distress and stayed in bed for a week.

Loss

Intimately involved in the experience of political violence are many emotionally charged processes concerned mainly with loss. Some individuals mourned the loss of limbs, normal bodily function, bodily health, or even a life.

A woman expressed her amazement at the sudden loss of her son:

My son was an orphan. . . . I educated him and he ranked first in the Faculty of Science. He studied mathematics and computer sciences. And in moments they finished him . . . they killed him.

One man mourned the loss of his son and the losses of relatives:

My family consists of thirteen members. My two brothers were imprisoned for three and a half years. And one day the private forces entered the house and took another brother and beat him [along] with twenty-eight other men. They were all treated in the hospital and discharged, except for a young man and my brother, who lost consciousness for six months. I had to accompany my brother to the hospital because all my brothers were in jail. I was the only one left to support the three families of my brothers, and my family was the fourth. In February 1993 my son was shot and killed; he was fifteen and one-half years old: THANK GOD, . . . my brother is alive, but mentally and physically handicapped as a result of the political violence during the *intifada;* he cannot be cured.

The experience of the traumatic event often became associated with economic loss, as two men reported:

I also was shot in the leg and I spent a considerable amount of time in the hospital and in centers. And now I cannot work because I am handicapped. The approximate percentage of the motor disability in my leg is 80 percent.

We don't have work permits, the Authority does not satisfy our needs by providing job opportunities and Israel does not give the ex-detainees permission to work. . . . How are we to eat?

Some parents had difficulty in healing from a mourned loss since their children had not been actively engaged in the *intifada* prior to their martyrdom but were picked up at random or by mistake. Such an especially poignant loss was described by the mother of a young boy:

> My son was standing at the window and a bullet entered his head. He could not say, "Save me, my mother," and my shock was very great; I can't express the severity of my pain. The young men took him to the hospital, but when we came back they forbade us from entering our houses, so they took his body for an autopsy. They brought him back in a garbage bag and allowed only twenty people to attend his funeral. We buried him in the middle of the night. And the effect of the trauma was very great and cannot be described, and all the money in the world cannot compensate for our loss, especially as it happened in front of our eyes.

Similarly, another mother told of the loss of her son:

> The soldiers asked my son to come to them, and when he reached them they shot him instantly. The day before . . . his leg had been hurting him as a result of a football game. I had gone downtown and when I came back I heard that my son had been martyred. . . . What was his guilt, to be killed while walking in the street without doing anything or hurting anybody?

Alienation and Neglect

Regardless of the specific configuration of cause and effect, it is clear that neglect was one of the themes that emerged in participants' discussions. The prevalent feeling was of having been abandoned by others. Most frequently, men and women expressed a hurt feeling toward the Authority, resulting from their disappointment and the violation of their expectations. This feeling of alienation also encompassed meaninglessness, power-lessness, normlessness, isolation, and self-estrangement.

The following quotations demonstrate feelings of being ne-glected and forsaken, feelings of detachment and estrangement from others, and the sense of a foreshortened future:

> I am the mother of a martyr, and the mother of people who suffered seven injuries in my house, and a widow . . . and no one shook hands with me . . . nobody entered my house on the feast of God . . . nobody remembers anybody . . . each one looks only to himself. . . . I told them on the feast day, "You don't shake hands with the mother of a martyr." There are no compliments for the mother of a martyr, they don't value the martyr or the prisoner . . . and they don't care for anybody. . . . Why is this our condition? Is this our Author-ity? What hopes do we have? . . . Are we hoping for any good from them? . . . When they came we received them ululating, we received them by dancing . . . thinking they would bring us good.

> Nobody feels with the affected people; nobody visits us. . . . Why don't they visit us and see our needs, and feel with us? Our children gave their lives and others got the positions and salaries, and we die every day and nobody hears us.

> We were exposed to all kinds of harm and the burdens were on our shoulders. Through our loss and suffering the Au-thority's men live in luxury, and the suffering and the sacri-fice of the people are the cause of their existence, but now they don't give any consideration to the martyrs or to any affected people. . . . Why is there not any shrine erected in honor of our martyrs? Or any celebration when people go out in recognition of the martyrs?

Secondary Victimization

Secondary victimization was one of the themes that emerged in participants' discussions. They referred to the many injustices that occurred to them after the crises. Many family members indicated that these secondary victimizations were, in fact, more painful in many ways than the actual crises because they were inflicted by others who were in caregiving roles and who recognized their vulnerability and abused them nonetheless. They also felt victimized by the systems they thought were put in place to relieve pain, not enhance it. The following six extracts reveal aspects of this theme:

> Ah, what can I tell you? What happened to me is not a minor thing. I am the mother of the martyr "M," who was shot in the stomach by the Israelis and was taken to America and died; and the mother of "H," the injured, who was shot in one eye, and in the other eye he doesn't see more than 30 percent; and the mother of "N," who was taken by the military army more than twenty times for interrogation, beatings, and humiliation; and my son "R" was in the Israeli prisons. But now they are in the prisons of the Authority. What can I tell you . . . about being beaten, or having my house broken into, or my humiliation by the military occupation? But whatever the Israelis do, like killing or terrorizing, I don't think of them . . . even if they shoot me or injure me or kill me. But now the Authority has come to complete their work for the Israelis . . . that's what kills me more than the killing of my children.

> They beat my son, the brother of a martyr, and the beating was very painful. I went to a person in the Palestinian Intelligence and I introduced myself as the mother of the martyr "I" and said that I spoke on behalf of the mothers of all the martyrs, and I told them, "When you came, we were very

happy and thought it would be for our good, but what you do now is more difficult to endure than what the Israelis did. Why do you beat my son when we are with you? If you are against us, we will be against you. The Israeli killed my son because I am his enemy, but why do you beat my son?"

That is what we got . . . the son of the poor became the bridge and they climbed over him. The son of the poor became the bridge for the son of the rich to pass over him, and they are the rich class and we are the poor class.

In the past our morale was high . . . let me tell you why . . . because the Israelis used to beat the women and the girls— but now you see your cousin . . . whom are you going to fight? Your brother . . . your cousin, these never threw a stone at the enemy; they used to hide in their houses . . . and now they have become responsible and they earn a salary at the expense of my son.

After they demolished our house, I built another house from my effort. The salary of "M" was not given to me, and I myself used to help the laborers in building the house. My suffering from this cannot be described. I found out that somebody took the salary of my son and has never given it to me.

Our house was demolished . . . and our neighbor, the one who builds houses, stole the stones. . . . Why does he steal the stones of our house? . . . This affected me psychologically to a great extent.

Support Resources

Support resources was a central theme that emerged in group discussions. Many men and women indicated that they did not get the support they expected and needed. Their perceptions of received support were based on actual experiences, as related by two men, one of whom was disappointed in the unavailability of both institutional and individual support:

> When we go to the institutions and societies they refuse to give us help, and they clearly say that they can't give any help.

> Believe me, they imprisoned my four sons, and one of them was sentenced to life in prison, and I don't remember that any institution or individual gave us help.

Some respondents, such as the woman quoted next, described ways in which institutions can give help, emphasizing the urgent need for helping afflicted families:

> Institutions can help in giving money or food . . . the welfare department does not give us any help, claiming that there is an employee in the family even though the number of family members is eighteen. But the injured, and the imprisoned, and the students need money to spend. My son, a student, does not have a *sheqel* to take with him to school. . . . He left school for this reason, although he is among the first in his class, and he is in the *tawjihi* (school leaving certificate year) class. He does not have money for a haircut or to buy clothes . . . and this is an example of my suffering.

Another woman, expressing a feeling of loneliness and a loss of the sense of solidarity, said:

> The affected person suffers alone, nobody helps, and especially from the morale side. Since 1985, I have been suffering from shock and confrontation. Even the solidarity of the people was not as expected . . . some institutions did not open for us because they were afraid, and we used to sit-in for the

sake of the prisoners in Jerusalem . . . they were suffering a great deal from beatings, persecution, and from bad health conditions . . . and that requires people to sit-in . . . but a lot of people did not come . . . this adds to my suffering. The relatives rarely ask . . . and when they do, it is verbal but nobody does anything.

The availability of resources, on the other hand, may contribute more to distress than to relief, when they do not function appropriately, as one man noted:

The societies and the medical charitable organizations do not help us. The doctors did not give the medical treatment needed by my brother who is handicapped and sick, and who needs a great deal of medical care.

In addition to the paucity of financial, moral, and medical support, complaints were raised regarding various concerns, and a number of criticisms of social support were made:

- My son, who is blind, was not rehabilitated by the local institutions such as the "Y," and he did not go to the Israeli institutions either.
- My son is handicapped and there is nobody who helped him to start a small project in order to support his family.
- The Authority does not give us any help.
- Nobody gives help. It is only talk, and more talk.
- We have not seen any good results.
- Nobody asks about anybody.
- Nobody cares.

Some respondents talked about the benefits and costs associated with the support provided. Although the intention of some of the support providers was to help, the outcome was not always perceived as beneficial for some affected members, which, in turn, has influenced their response to seeking social support.

Expressing the financial costs she incurred, one woman related:

> They invited "A" to a festival in Ramallah for the support of the injured. We took a cab for "A" to go to Ramallah. It cost NIS 100. They received "A" and they gave him a medal and 50 Jordanian dinars. We paid NIS 100, and all that was left for us was NIS 100. And then he was invited to Hebron, and it cost us NIS 70 to get him there . . . they gave him a medal and NIS 70, and when I went to cash the check, they told me that it had to be cashed in Hebron, and I paid NIS 14 for the transportation, so I paid more than the value of what was given to him.

Another woman mentioned the insuffiency of help given:

> The social welfare department gives us NIS 79 per month; this is what they will do for us; I don't do any work on that day for NIS 79.

Still another talked about her social anxiety, which involved feeling awkward, discomfited, and exposed because of her situation:

> I went to "C" for help and told the social worker that my two sons were in prison, each one sentenced for ten years. She asked the names and I gave them to her. I asked for help but I was embarrassed. They said, "We have to see your house." After two weeks, two employees from "C" came and they saw that our condition was difficult. They asked me to go and visit them, and I went. She gave me a receipt for NIS 100. She said, "You can spend it in your town." This was a monthly support, but after six months, they stopped giving it, and then I asked again, and they said, "Come after the new year." In a month, I went back and they refused to

help. All this was not worth my effort and the embarrassment that I faced.

Some of the "support themes" questioned motives for giving help; the uncertainty surrounding support, with resulting mistrust, emerged strongly in the following three statements:

> Some of the institutions came to us, such as the "O." They filled out questionnaires and forms and asked routine questions such as who lives in the house and their ages, the number of boys and the number of girls, the family income . . . they used to take pictures of the martyr, but until now we have not received anything from the institutions. Another institution, "Z," did the same as "O," and they never came back; they also took a picture of the youngest girl and of the martyr. They asked the name of the family, the house rent, expenditures, and income, and a lot of institutions did the same and we never got anything from them. A lot of institutions were doing data collection only, and they never gave help . . . all that we got was the scandal and their behavior, as if they were doing us a favor. They used to say that their institution went to the house of the father of that martyr and that prisoner. But the actual help was never given to us by the institutions that were appointed to give the help.

> These institutions come for the sake of help, but they collect data for the sake of financial embezzlement.

> I sold my wife's gold in order to treat my son, and I went to the institutions for help, but I believe that the money for help is taken and stolen by certain people who did not participate in the *intifada*.

A theme was raised concerning how provider variables, relationship variables, and sociocultural variables may have affected support provision. Support providers seemed to be affected by the nature of the relationship with the support recipients and by background sociocultural factors. Perhaps the firmest statement on relationship factors that related to support provision involved affiliation with a political party. Many of the respondents recalled with considerable pain the discrimination and differentness they experienced in receiving support. The following four extracts demonstrate this:

- The Authority should come to the house of "L" and tell him, "Here is your salary" and tell him that you gave and struggled. The Authority should not differentiate between a person who belongs to the Popular Front, Fateh, or who is a Communist.
- The support should be given to everybody without any political discrimination.
- The institutions are there, but the support is given to friends and relatives.
- There are institutions that give some help, but they differentiate and discriminate and they prefer some people over others. The institutions that belonged to the Authority filled out questionnaires and promised to give us help . . . but we did not see anything, but there are people who received help.

Some participants had trauma-related beliefs salient to support. One belief was that "nobody will help" because of fear of association. Several men indicated that people's fear of being hurt was compounded by difficulties in providing support:

I have a brother who was killed in a military operation. And because of his affiliation with Hammas and after the imprisonment of so many people, we found out that there is fear among people that prevents them from offering help. They

are afraid of being accused of being followers of Hammas
. . . which means there is an obstacle to giving help.

No . . . even for people who don't belong to Hammas the
help is not given, and the proof is that when they start to
distribute Al-Zaka money for the poor and the needy families, the Israeli authorities put their hands on any person
who distributes Al-Zaka, and claim that he is a follower of
Hammas, and accuse him of distributing the money to the
military of Hammas.

The religious people don't help . . . everybody is afraid,
even the Palestinian Authority, the institutions, and the social welfare department.

I might like to help a brother who is in a situation similar to
mine, but I am afraid that the Israeli authority will put me in
jail because of this help.

Several men talked about the changes in the extended family
and community ties in terms of support and interpersonal relationships:

In the past the Israeli authority demolished four houses, and
as a result, all the Hamoulas in the city collected money to
build houses for the four dispossessed families. But now-
adays there is no help, because they are afraid of any ac-
cusation.

These days we have coldness and indifference. In the past
when a bride's car passed, everybody used to sing, clap, and
dance with them, but now there is no feeling for interaction.
I, for example, had my house demolished twenty months
ago and I live in a tent, and no one has yet knocked on my
door to offer help, either from societies, institutions, or the
Authority.

Some respondents indicated their need for support that might help them cope with stresses associated with crises such as un-employment or lack of housing:

- They should look into the needs of the affected families and find job opportunities for them; we are such as prisoners under the closure of the territories, and nobody feels with the affected people.
- In my opinion, all these people who were affected should be given the help needed to start a productive project.
- The most important thing is to build houses for those who had their houses demolished . . . to provide a place to live.
- It is important to provide my handicapped son with all that he needs, so he will not go on the street and the people will not feel disgusted with him.

Self-Esteem

Support often poses a conflict between one's self-image and the behavior that is deemed necessary for survival. Self-esteem was a fundamental aspect that intervened in the relationship between the acceptance of help and the self-ideal that was shaped by certain values to which some people aspired, as in the case of these three men:

- I don't ask for financial help because this is humiliating for the martyr, and this giving is for the country.
- I am the father of the martyr "B." I have three martyrs in the family, but I refuse financial support.
- I am from the old fighters of the revolution, and I refuse to take anything in return for my sacrifice for the country.

Appraisal and Coping

Many individuals described the strategies they employed while confronted with their crises. No one strategy or combination of strategies was used by all family members under extreme conditions. However, the discussion revolved around four dimensions of appraisal and coping. The line of thought followed by the majority of the inflicted family members leads us to consider the possibility that ideology is a resource that mediates the impact of political traumas by influencing the coping process. In essence, beliefs and commitments manifest forbearance under provocation, strain, and adversity, and, in consequence, are conducive to enduring pain:

- We are steadfast and we remain steadfast because Palestine is precious, our land and our country. This thing runs in our blood. When my sister's son was killed, she knelt and kissed the ground, and she said, "Thank God that 'N' was killed as a sacrifice for Palestine."
- Our children were working for the benefit of our country, and we are convinced they were right, and that is why we bear everything and stand fast.
- The martyrdom of every Palestinian youth is a source of pride. The massacre in the Abraham mosque was twenty-five months ago; it was an act of revenge . . . but my feelings from the beginning were of happiness because my son was killed in honor and not for theft.

Many participants expressed resigned acceptance, which included such responses as being patient because there was no alternative:

My son went to Yugoslavia for treatment because of his injury during the *intifada* and we did not hear from him. The army raided the house and took my second child . . . so what can we do except be patient?

For some, resigned acceptance was expressed overtly, suggesting its roots in powerful religious beliefs:

- What is written by God is going to happen, and we thank God for any situation.
- I face my problems with faith, patience, and praying.
- I read the Koran.

Appraisal-focused coping was another coded category that emerged in the group sessions. This category included cognitive redefinition strategies by which people accepted the reality of the situation but restructured it to find something favorable, such as thinking of oneself with respect to other people:

> Whoever sees the catastrophes of others finds that his catastrophe becomes easier.

> My brothers, when I see the soldiers coming at night to imprison my children . . . we all find it difficult, but in the end I compare my situation with the situation of others who are in the same boat, so I say I am not better than the others, and the catastrophes of others are more difficult.

Some men and women described how they handled the emotions aroused by their crises and thereby maintained effective equilibrium. Typical responses included emotional discharge expressions such as screaming and crying. Both men and women experienced such catharsis:

> I entered the room and hid under the bed after my son had been killed by the Israeli Army; then I closed the doors and windows in order not to let any of the neighbors hear me, and I started screaming and crying in order to cope with my disaster, and used this to comfort me psychologically and help me to overcome the problem.

> We used to be sad and cry and neglect ourselves . . . we did not comb our hair for a week . . . everybody was sad and the sad atmosphere prevailed.

> You can imagine how I felt about that . . . when I was standing and with my own eyes I saw a soldier in a bulldozer demolishing my house . . . or taking my son from my lap.

One man, however, faced victimization only by blaming his son for their situation:

> I became angry with my son because he was the cause of the demolishing of the house.

Value Changes

Change of values was one of the themes that emerged in group discussions. It seems that political traumas had serious repercussions on family values and on the deeply engrained standards that determined directions and justified actions in Palestinian society. The overwhelming impact of traumas on changing values was either explicitly discussed or implied in focus group discussions. Even transitions in the socially defined women's roles, which, in principle, involve the risk of a breakdown, come to be routinized and even taken for granted. Political crises are conceived as turning points, or social "passages," in the lives of Palestinian family members; they indicate transformation from what one "ought" to do to what one "wants" to do.

One man expressed the traditional respect of a husband for his wife:

> If they give you 1,000 Jordanian dinars to let your wife go out on the street after midnight, I am sure that you will not accept that . . . but rather to allow our wives to do so in order to be able to visit their sons in prison and in order to be able to take the Jewish bus and reach the prison, at the time of the visit.

Implied in most of the group discussions was the active role of women in the political struggle. This was brought out explicitly in the following two statements made by women:

My daughter was injured in the waist and she had three operations, and my son was injured in the leg and was imprisoned several times . . . and then he was martyred and my injured daughter was put in jail, and I was injured in the arm . . . and during the Israeli occupation I had seven sons in prison, and my daughter is the eighth child . . . and I didn't know where to go, to the prison of Alfar'a, or Jenin, or Nablus, or Hebron.

I spent three months looking for my son; I had a lawyer and after three months he told me that my son needed a witness because he had a court marshal. So I took "K," who had just had a baby twenty days before. The lawyer told me that my son could not come to court because he was sick . . . and when he told me that my son was sick, and that I had to pay bail, I stood in the middle of the courtroom, and in front of me there were three judges, . . . I said, "I don't give Kessef [money] for the Jews." . . . I said it in Hebrew so that they would understand me . . . the rascals came to my house and took my son while he was eating and he stayed in the hospital three months . . . and now they want me to give them money. The translator told me to shut up . . . and I told him, "I am not in the house of your father, I am in the court and I want to say what I want."

Others talked about the transformation of other social processes:

In the past support was stronger . . . but after peace it was weakened. In the past the support used to reach us under all conditions . . . when there were curfews . . . and when we were under siege, but now this doesn't occur anymore.

Need for Recognition

One of the important themes raised was the need for recognition. Official recognition seems to have psychological meaning. Many family members expressed the essential need to be recognized and respected. This was not simply self-recognition, but recognition of others, as forcefully stated by these two women:

> The father of "L," . . . they should put a medal of honor in front of his house, and the father of "M," they should give him a medal of honor. . . . I am from one end of the camp, and he is from the other end, but I see him dragging his legs . . . I am saying what's true . . . and when I see him I have a wound in my heart . . . he sits on a chair all day long.

> The Authority should provide a place for the martyrs where people can put their pictures and sayings . . . for the sake of the martyrs and their families.

Needs, Demands, and Rights

Group discussions revolved around family members' needs, demands, and rights. Their demands implied peremptoriness, insistence, and often rights to make requests from Authority, community, and significant others. This imperativeness arose from their inner necessity and from their experiences with traumatic situations. Much of the focus in the discussion was on socioeconomic and political issues. The following statements are typical of the discussions on this theme:

- I think that the Authority should start projects in order to provide more job opportunities for our children.
- The political parties have to provide the injured with work in order to earn a living and get what they need.
- Work should be provided for the unemployed.

- The institutions have to provide work and education for our children who were harmed.
- I will feel much better if my children are released from prison.
- Ah, if I could build a house and get a job.
- I wish that the prisoners were released and the injured cured and that God would compensate for the ones who were killed.
- The Authority has to provide the medical insurance, housing, education, and other demands for the families of those who were killed, imprisoned, and injured.

SECTION II: POSTTRAUMA ENVIRONMENT AND RECOVERY

Political violence and oppression are problems of monumental proportion in the West Bank and Gaza Strip. Palestinian families have sustained multiple losses, including both tangible and internal ones. As is apparent in narratives, family members identified prominent affects and affective states (e.g., fear, loss, anger), salient cognitive sequelae (e.g., negative schemata about people), and interpersonal difficulties (e.g., isolation, alienation).

The reactions of society at large to the affected family members have a significant negative effect on posttrauma adaptation and the ability to integrate the traumatic experiences. Clearly, subtle or dramatic changes occur, a sense of aliveness may be temporarily or even permanently lost, and feelings and beliefs about the self and others deplete those traumatized individuals of meaning and vitality.

The negative feelings of family members, created by traumatic conditions during the military occupation, are reinforced by other hideous experiences in the new sociopolitical order. The traumatic experiences of confronting death, demolition of houses, imprisonment, and physical injuries, followed by injustices, alienation, and neglect, are deeply imprinted on the memory of afflicted family members and may accompany them throughout their lives.

Psychological responses described in group discussions are protean. They include depression, anxiety, fear, somatization, sleeplessness due to nightmares and other intrusive phenomena, social withdrawal, and helplessness.

The range of symptoms expressed is very wide, including features of many of the common psychiatric conditions experienced by victims of political violence (Allodi and Cowgill, 1982; Rasmussen and Lunde, 1980; Turner and Gorst-Unsworth, 1993). Many family members continued to have intrusive distressing recollections of the events without any external triggering stimulus. These painful images and recollections are difficult to deal with in posttrauma adaptations.

The process of adaptation is facilitated by a stable and supportive environment. The lack of support is therefore likely to prolong grief and impair adaptation (Bonan and Eduards, 1984; Wardak, 1988, 1993). The negative consequences of traumatization could be counteracted (or augmented) through satisfactory (or dissatisfactory) experiences within the contexts of family, social network, and community. It is through relationships and social support in these contexts that individuals establish and maintain a sense of meaning and purpose in their lives. Social support, however, is likely to be undermined under conditions of traumatic stress (Kahana, Midlarsky, and Kahana, 1987).

Paralleling the psychological sequelae of state-sponsored violence is equally pervasive damage caused by secondary victimization. Symonds (1980) coined this postvictimization period, in which victims come to perceive themselves as rejected by the community, its agencies, and society in general as the "secondary injury" to victims. Although the themes identified in this analysis appeared in many different forms among the affected family members, a pattern of interconnections was evident after men and women described explicitly when their pain and social suffering were overlooked, minimized, or even ignored. Secondary victimizations are very painful for Palestinian family members because these injuries are often inflicted by people they have decided to trust and to view as protectors (Authority). Pain was inflicted when they were treated as appendages of a system appallingly out of balance. They soon discovered that their previous expectations of the Authority would not be fulfilled in terms of providing support and adopting a responsible attitude toward those who sacrificed and who were victimized. From an interpersonal perspective, the emotional construction of oneself as a passive victim in a world of malevolent others may lead to feelings and interactions with others that sustain feelings of anxiety, depression, and negative self-esteem (Strupp and Binder, 1984).

A prevailing notion that came out of group discussions was that, in addition to alienation, neglect, and secondary victimization, an in-group and out-group bias was salient. It is a truism that the majority of the people in the West Bank and Gaza Strip began to form perceptions of themselves as "the group who were steadfast and suffered," and that Palestinians and organizations external to the traumatic events that were not on the scene from the beginning became an out-group because they did not share the afflicted family members' emotional experiences and common social identity; they are often evaluated in comparison to central values such as political suffering. Such differentiation and greater division into in- and out-groups is sufficient for the creation of intergroup discrimination, even in disastrous situations (Turner, 1982). Family members described with remarkable eloquence that large segments of the families affected during the *intifada* now lack access to adequate levels of basic goods and services because they are not affiliated with or do not belong to the dominant political party, and because they do not possess unconditional rights to gainful employment and adequate income.

The debilitating consequences of unemployment, poverty, and downward mobility; the inequality of competition for employment, promotions, preferred positions, conditions, and opportunities; as well as marginalization and nonrecognition of the families' sacrifices frustrate the realization of the material and psychological needs of many Palestinian family members, thereby inhibiting their posttrauma recovery. Few family members can be expected to develop a genuine sense of security, and, indeed, many suffer a nagging sense of insecurity.

The overall social change and shift in values produced by the posttrauma culture play a significant role in the prolonged grief and maladaptation of family members. Variations in gender roles have increased, and traditional values are being questioned. Some of the family members referred to women's roles that were influenced by a variety of political factors. Particular emphasis has been given to the involuntary changes in social norms for gender role behavior. Political traumas, however, may have offered women opportunities to gain control that were not available in their traditional roles, whereby men's tensions seem likely to surface. On the other hand, the absence of men in the Palestinian households (e.g., men imprisoned, killed) may have burdened women with the dual responsibilities of productive and family roles and of assuming men's responsibilities as economic providers and political activists and fighters.

A noteworthy trend discernible in the data is that the majority of family members were not satisfied with the provision and receipt of social support, had mistrust and doubts about motives for helping, lacked sociofamilial cohesiveness and support in the immediate aftermath of a catastrophe, and therefore did not perceive themselves as receiving the support to which they are entitled. Often, under conditions of traumatic stress, social supports are likely to be undermined (Kahana, Midlansky, and Kahana, 1987). However, the conceptions of the need for help held by some family members may conflict. Receiving help and seeking help may be interpreted as a negative or unfavorable reflection on one's own abilities. From an attributional perspective, when receiving help becomes a norm, this normativeness can directly affect the attribution process. Thus, if the persons receiving help believe that everyone in a similar situation needs help, they would not doubt their own abilities or suffer a loss of self-esteem (Eranen and Liebkind, 1993).

Nonetheless, the majority of the family members who focused in their discussion on their need for social resources reflected aspects of instrumental support rather than socioemotional support. They emphasized their urgent need for financial assistance, concrete and tangible services, whereas the value of socioemotional support was understated in their discussion. It has been argued that the opportunity for intimacy and fulfillment of expressive needs improves the individual's ability to deal with crises (Dean and Lin, 1977), and that socioemotional support helps to maintain a sense of self and facilitates coping (Thoits, 1983). It would seem that the type and amount of support needed by affected Palestinian families is proportionate to the amount by which expansiveness of life is curtailed.

One of the most salient aspects of the social support thematic analysis was people's fear of support. The fear of providing support to the affected family members was engendered by oppression. This type of abuse appears to be closely associated with views of oneself as relatively powerless vis-à-vis powerful others who are capable of political persecution. The images of self and others that emerged in the interpersonal discussion revealed close associations among the fear of power, feelings of personal powerlessness and helplessness, and a sense of significant others as untrustworthy. The Authority was consistently depicted in a more negative light than it had been before it came to power.

However, social support requires both a personal initiative and a socioenvironmental response. The content analysis of the traumatic response patterns of affected family members provided important descriptive information that may explain the hypothesis of ideology as a buffer of stress. Cognitive appraisal of stressful situations is regarded as a very important factor in determining stress and anxiety responses (Lazarus, 1966; Lazarus and Folkman, 1984). It seems that Palestinians' politicoreligious beliefs (*jihad* and *shahadah*), and love and commitment to their homeland, influenced their appraisal by shaping their understanding of exposure to political violence and, in consequence, their emotions and coping efforts related to the traumatic experience.

Specific cognitive-focused coping patterns regarding response to traumas were evident in focus group discussions. These coping styles are culturally prescribed and learned within the Palestinian cultural and subcultural contexts. They encompass cognitive avoidance responses aimed at accepting a situation as it is, and therefore exercising patience because the basic circumstances are difficult to alter, or else attributing problems to external factors that are beyond one's control, that is, the will of God.

Other responses included venting one's feelings through emotional discharges such as crying. This coping style was observed more among women, and that may be consistent with the norms of female behavior in Palestinian culture.

Chapter 5

Conclusions
and an Agenda for Action

In this book, I have addressed several major problems that confront families who have sustained *intifada*-related traumas that have resulted in varying degrees of stress. These problems are psychological, political, institutional, and interpersonal, and they vary from family to family according to its social structure, political identity, and socioeconomic status, while also being predictable and unpredictable. Despite this variability, several recurring themes have implications for identification, prevention, intervention, and social policy analysis. This final chapter presents an integrative summary of these major themes, including (1) psychological sequelae of political traumas; (2) prevention and intervention considerations; (3) institutional injustice; (4) social support mediators; (5) sociopolitical mediators; (6) social policy; and (7) research implications.

PSYCHOLOGICAL SEQUELAE
OF POLITICAL TRAUMAS

The study has documented that approximately 35 percent of the Palestinian families who were subjected to political violence qualify as having a history of PTSD and that the disorder has a heterogeneous course, with excess risk for chronic symptoms and comorbidity with other disorders. Also, family members with high levels of trauma-related stress suffer from substantial current rates of other mental health disorders (e.g., depression, cognitive disturbance, anxiety). The high rates of PTSD and psychiatric disorders are attributed to living under conditions of constant political oppression, overwhelming experiences of death and destruction, and excessive demands. Nonetheless, the risk for PTSD varies by type of trauma and proximity to the traumatic event. Having a family member killed confers the highest risk, whereas having a family member imprisoned rarely leads to PTSD. Also, the conditional risk of PTSD, given exposure to trauma, is approximately twofold higher in direct victims, such as the injured of the *intifada* (Khamis, 1993a), than in indirect victims (family members of the injured). Other risk factors for PTSD include individual characteristics and environmental aspects.

Clearly, intense psychological distress and psychosocial maladjustment may persist for many years following extreme forms of political violence (Khamis, 1993b). Many of the afflicted family members had trauma-induced stress within the various dimensions of their lives, particularly strains in health, work, marriage, and family relationships. In addition, a variety of role strains have been experienced by family members as a result of the traumatic events, such as strains that are generated by the occupancy of multiple roles, role reversals (e.g., loss and gain of roles), interrole conflict, increased role demands regarding finances and supply, parenting, and care for those who were injured and sustained a disability. The most obvious strains are increased role obligations in parenting, homemaking, satisfying spousal needs, and helping children with schoolwork.

PREVENTION AND INTERVENTION CONSIDERATIONS

With the recognition of the psychological damage and the associated stressors that follow political traumas among Palestinians, there should be a growing concern among mental health professionals to prevent or minimize posttraumatic morbidity. However, some issues are particularly salient in hindering the therapeutic process. These issues will raise questions about the traumatized individuals, the mental health professionals, the delivery of psychological services, and the reliability of models of assessment and intervention. In general, family members seldom seek professional help to deal with the emotional impact of traumatic events. This may be due to the desire to avoid the stigma associated with mental health problems and/or the scarcity of counseling services and therapists in the West Bank and Gaza Strip. Most family members initially try to solve their psychological problems on their own, with the help of relatives, religious people, and traditional healers. They only ask for professional help when the problem escalates and brings with it additional crisis.

However, recent progress has been made. The increased recognition by mental health professionals of the long-term negative impact of political traumas has been a major impetus for the establishment of the rehabilitation centers in the West Bank and Gaza Strip (UNCTAD, 1994b). However, these services provide physiotherapy, prostheses, orthoses, and adaptive devices for the injured of the *intifada* who sustained physical disabilities. Approaches to recovery and treatment, such as intervention and psychotherapy, are lacking. Also, the assessment and treatment models used by the few professionals are based on Western standards, disregarding the cultural dimensions of Palestinian society. Many of these models are culturally insensitive and contradict clients' norms, mores, beliefs, and values. Despite the expressed concern for a comprehensive system for strategy formulation and planning of health care services in the West Bank and Gaza Strip, mental health care is barely considered. Many of the most crucial sources of psychopathology and human suffering have little place in policy development. Therefore, efforts to build systems of care will have to recognize the importance of psychological services in the identification, prevention, and intervention of mental health problems for victims of political violence.

Prevention approaches are necessary for the treatment of posttrauma mental health problems following political traumas. A number of prevention strategies have been discussed in the literature (Freedy and Donkervoet, 1995; Norris and Thompson, 1995) that distinguish between interventions taking place before the crisis (primary prevention), during the crisis (secondary prevention), or after the crisis (tertiary prevention). Optimal interventions focus on preventing trauma exposure and/or limiting negative mental health effects resulting from trauma exposure.

In the West Bank and Gaza Strip, two types of primary prevention may be suggested. First, it may be possible to reduce the number of political traumatic events through political activism directed at lessening the incidence of political violence and oppression. This may be realized through (1) programs or social policies that protect Palestinians or groups of individuals from the occurrence of institutional injustice and malpractice by those who are in power positions and (2) empowering Palestinians to deal constructively with interpersonal conflict, cultural differences, and intergroup conflict. This may be achieved through training workshops and educational programs aimed at conflict prevention, anger management, and relationship and community building. Also, primary prevention approaches such as stress-mitigation programs may be directed toward those who were seen as vulnerable, living in areas that are highly exposed to political violence, and to others who have certain statuses and roles, such as women, the elderly, and those of low socioeconomic status and with little education. Generic educational programs that provide information about normal responses, sources of help, and preventive and helpful measures are needed (Raphael and Wilson, 1993). A second key means of reducing traumatic events in the region is through peacemaking. However, the resolution of the Arab-Israeli conflict is best and most assuredly achieved through a solution that is mutually acceptable to all parties, self-sustaining in the long run, and productive of a new and positive lifestyle to be lived by both Palestinians and Israelis.

Secondary prevention efforts may include strategies that aim to expedite the recovery of individuals who have recently experienced a particular political trauma and/or to restore or provide access to system level resources. Numerous authors have (Bailey et al., 1985; Cohen, 1985) advocated the use of crisis intervention following disasters to prevent the development of psychopathology and have offered useful guidelines for such services. Such crisis counseling services were initiated during the *intifada* (Tamari, Kassis, and Khamis, 1989). However, these services had limitations in regard to the forms of assistance provided and the availability of trained professionals. Also, most of the services were focused on those handicapped during the *intifada*.

As a strategy for secondary prevention, community development is particularly appropriate. Efforts should be placed on mobilizing communities' capabilities and on helping the communities to become self-sufficient. Therefore, community intervention programs should be encouraged. These include didactic expositions of studies on Palestinian families, recommendations for action, and group discussions in which community members can share their experiences and problems (Fredrick, 1985; Rigamer, 1986).

Tertiary prevention may be provided through a wide range of psychological services, including individual therapy or counseling, group therapy, and family therapy. However, treatment will necessarily depend on local circumstances and should take into account the cultural background of the traumatized individuals (Badri, 1979; Kinzie, 1989; Vesti and Kastrup, 1992). These services require credentialed clinicians in psychiatry, psychology, and social work, as well as allied professionals, and, therefore, training programs and in-service workshops are urgently needed to teach people to catalog, evaluate, and refine a therapeutic armamentarium to serve traumatized family members.

Successful psychological treatment may be trauma focused, since several currently practiced treatment modalities require the person to focus on traumatic memories (Freedy and Donkervoet, 1995). Such treatment approaches range from implosive therapy (flooding) to cognitive therapies that encourage thinking and talking about the personal meaning of traumatic experiences (Lyons and Keane, 1989; Resick, 1992; Rothbaum and Foa, 1992).

INSTITUTIONAL INJUSTICE

An overwhelming finding in this book is the existence of an institutional context of injustice that far too often follows trauma. The lack of resources, alienation, neglect, and secondary victimization constitute some of the most effective mechanisms to ensure the traumas' continued impact on the affected family members. These findings raise the important question of whether the abuse and injustice is limited to the affected family members, or whether there is a general tendency for each group (e.g., religious, political) to have its disfavored group. Unfortunately, group categorization is socially constructed and inserted in a subtle way into the functional institutions of society.

The socioeconomic and political conditions in the West Bank and Gaza Strip have influenced the notion of social categories and defined the essential properties that maintain their mutual exclusivity. Thus, the response to institutional injustice is necessarily as complex as the political traumas themselves. However, the negative impact of such injustice on family members' psychological well-being dictates a political reform rather than merely professional interventions. Unconditional human rights laws should be established for all Palestinians, in general, and for victims of political violence, in particular. Legislation protective of the affected families may be initiated in a wide variety of services, such as provisions for mental health care, social welfare, and civil rights. Laws, legislation, and procedural measures must be enforced to accomplish revolutionary transformations. Such transformations require redesigning and reconstructing the economic, political, social, and cultural institutions in accordance with egalitarian, cooperative, and genuinely democratic values. Within this context, the Palestinian Authority is urged to generate sufficient political commitment and courage to promote normative change in Palestinian society. This is difficult, but its likelihood is increased if the institutional change toward diversity is inevitable. Behavioral change often leads to attitude change, and such change will eventually take place when the arsenal of efforts are directed to realize the Palestinian dream of real liberation.

SOCIAL SUPPORT MEDIATORS

Palestinians share a common thread of family-centered social support systems in which emotional, financial, and instrumental support is given. They operate within an extended family system in which resources are provided as support to immediate and extended kin relations. Families are therefore responsible for primary social and emotional support in which mutual obligation and reciprocity among members is expected. However, traumatic events often interfere with the normal functioning of social networks through the death of others, or through disruptions caused by responses to the events (Joseph, Williams, and Yule, 1997; McFarlane, 1988). Shalev (1996) points out that trauma profoundly alters the basic structure of the individual and cultural system in which it occurs. The homeostatic mechanisms of a society (e.g., rituals, social organization, and the economic system) no longer suffice to restore a sense of safety and belonging, and other forms of organizations or institutions need to take their place.

During the *intifada,* however, many Palestinian families have been exposed to political traumas that have caused tremendous losses of family resources (e.g., financial, emotional). These resources have been cut rapidly, broadly, and deeply, to the extent that the usual arsenal of family support responses may have failed to fulfill expectations for aid (Khamis, 1995a). After confronting initial resource loss, people have fewer or less potent resources for the additional challenges that come in the wake of the first loss circumstances (Hobfoll, Dunahoo, and Monnier, 1995). Also, the trauma-induced stress may contribute to a sequence of further losses, each attacking the affected families, which have ever-decreasing resources. Therefore, many affected families were incapable of doing their protective work and could not adequately fulfill their functions of regulating emotions, and of providing support and resources.

With the current political situation, further loss occurs, resulting in an increasing level of family vulnerability, as resources become further depleted. For example, the permit and border closure policies implemented by Israel since 1993 have substantially overburdened families' resource thresholds, as evidenced in lower income levels, greater unemployment, and increased poverty (Palestinian Economic Policy Research Institute MAS, 1998a). Under these circumstances, communality has increased and many nongovernmental organizations and institutions have become the potential providers of support in the West Bank and Gaza Strip. Also, political and religious organizations have become the backbone of the formal Palestinian support system, particularly with respect to their role in promoting instrumental support (e.g., financial). As a result, financial assistance has become the national norm for supportive relationships.

Family members' emphasis on financial support was a repeated theme in group discussions. The sociopolitical conditions of the Palestinians therefore provide the contextual grounding for social support to be given and received. This context allows for the expression of certain needs that would require providing social support. However, the politicoreligious identity of the affected family members, the shared belief system of the group, along with attitudes and expectations, also provide direction and guidance as to who receives social support. In many respects, financial support has been beneficial to those with group affiliations. Similar to all those whose needs go unmet over the long term, the affected family members feel victimized. Although it would be an oversimplification to attribute all the problems to unequal distribution of resources within the social system, this imbalance certainly makes a significant contribution. Whenever one group meets its own needs at the expense of another, the stage is set for stress and conflict that, in turn, may hinder the process of recovery.

Identifying variants in support resources may help us to allocate social interventions logically. There is no doubt that certain types of support resources moderate the response to political traumas. For example, high levels of support from institutions and significant others were found to be associated with lower levels of role strains among the affected family members, whereas high levels of support from religious and political groups were found to be associated with less psychiatric symptomatology. The perception is that social support interventions should be based on careful assessment of a family's psychosocial history, past and present losses and stressors, and the family's patterns of interaction. This assessment is important for predicting the appropriateness and effectiveness of various social support interventions.

A wide range of intervention programs may be developed to increase the social support of the affected family members. Since traumatic events tend to disrupt the role of family provider, family members may need to be encouraged and assisted in locating resources for social support outside the nuclear family (Green and Solomon, 1995). These resources may include self-help groups tailored to particular victim groups, such as groups for families who had a family member killed or injured. Other interventions may consist of social skills training or restructuring social environments. Social skills training targets skill deficits in low-social-support individuals (Sarason et al., 1985). For example, the skills training programs may target skill deficits in low-social-support individuals, helping develop the personal qualities needed to improve their own naturally occurring relationships. The intervention may focus on a wide range of social, cognitive, and behavioral skills, scheduled group activities, and network development. The main components of the program may focus on the common problem areas of affected family members, such as problem solving, making positive social contacts, requesting help, and improving the quality of family patterns of interaction.

Further investigation of the mechanisms through which social support affects traumatized family members is needed. Furthermore, both quantitative and qualitative methods should be developed to study the range of issues in understanding social support in contemporary Palestinian society. Areas to be studied may include support schemata, supportive relationships, and supportive interactions. These elements of the social support construct are not exclusive; they overlap and influence one another in important ways (Pierce et al., 1996). Also, an essential aspect that may need to be investigated is the perceptual biases that may contribute to perceived social support (Lakey and Lutz, 1996), since perceptual biases might be affected by group affiliations.

SOCIOPOLITICAL MEDIATORS

An important class of mediators of psychological responses to political traumas relates to the sociopolitical context of the affected family members. Sociopolitical factors that potentially affect family members' responses include the degree of satisfaction with the political situation, work, and social life.

The sociopolitical conditions of the West Bank and Gaza Strip present formidable obstacles to the achievement of positive well-being among Palestinians. Unfortunately, the quality of life is much less than was the case before the Declaration of Principles in the Oslo accord, signed by the State of Israel and the Palestinian Liberation Organization in September 1993. As an integral part of Palestinian society, the family members were also affected, suffering from political uncertainties, economic deterioration, and inadequate standards of living and social life (MAS, 1998b). Most of the affected families are coping with some problems in their daily lives that are associated per se with a traumatic event. The structural changes that have taken place in families as a result of deaths, disabilities, and imprisonment have contributed to increased stress levels. However, the level of stress experienced by affected families, similar to that experienced by families from the mainstream population in the West Bank and Gaza Strip, appears to be increasing because of political uncertainties. In addition, families are also experiencing a decrease in economic well-being, including employment instability and downward mobility (MAS, 1998a,b).

The UNCTAD (1994a) document indicated that the unemployment rate, which was officially reported at around 2 percent of the labor force in 1987, and otherwise estimated at 10 to 12 percent of the 1990 labor force, would reach some 50 percent of the labor force by the year 2010 in the West Bank and Gaza Strip. The Palestinian Central Bureau of Statistics estimates that the rate of unemployment was 18.2 percent in September to October 1995, and 28.4 percent in April to May 1996. Approximately 20.1 percent of the population in the West Bank and Gaza Strip lives below the poverty line (Diwan and Radwan, 1999). Therefore, it is recommended that a relief program, designed to aid the affected families of the unemployed, be initiated to ease their postrecovery adjustment.

Although unemployment is the most pressing problem at present, there is a call to create an institutional framework to support affected family members and improve their access to credit, financial, and legal assistance. Since many of the families faced death, imprisonment, or injury of male members, some considerations should be given to the inclusion of women and the disabled in economic life. Therefore, it is important to embark on a general campaign aimed at mobilizing women and the disabled, enhancing awareness of their rights in employment opportunities, and ensuring equal pay and chances of promotion.

The outlook for employment of women and the disabled may be improved dramatically through legislation, research, and pilot programs. The Palestinian Authority is encouraged to work on an act or legislation that requires reasonable accommodation to create equal employment opportunities for people who sustained injuries and also for women who lost an economic provider. Vocational training for these people is resulting in more personal independence, economic self-sufficiency, and social acceptance. Specific consideration in research should be given to surveying the community for jobs, identifying and analyzing the requisite skills of potential employment sites, providing systematic training in job-related skills, and providing follow-up training and maintenance of learned skills. Therefore, the Palestinian Authority faces many challenges in formulating policies and adopting strategies and projects to enable and ensure both peace and development in the midst of political and economic constraints. A coordinated series of efforts should be directed toward improving the sociopolitical situation and providing a focus for rehabilitative work in family networks, institutions, and communities.

SOCIAL POLICY

The rights and needs of victims of political violence may present a special problem for public policy as it relates to conflict over the nature of the problems confronting Palestinian society and the priority of needs. Ideally, social policy ought to be rational if the ratio between the values it achieves and the values it sacrifices is positive and higher than any other alternative policy. A political action ought to be rational when it is directed explicitly at reducing the incidence of stressful life events among afflicted family members. According to Kessler and Albee (1975), the prevention of psychosocial problems requires the abolition of social injustices such as employment discrimination and poverty. Mental health professionals have difficulty working on affected family members' posttrauma recovery, for example, when the situational determinants of posttrauma recovery, such as having employment, social support, or living in a just world, are not in place. Undoubtedly, an urgent need exists for a broadbased governmental response that includes the enactment of appropriate legislation, justice system reform, and extensive community education programs. In fact, the laws applied by the Palestinian Authority are very old and were adopted from previous rules: the Ottoman, the British, followed by the Jordanian. The symbolic and practical importance of a Palestinian Authority policy in molding the behavior of officials toward the Palestinian people, in general, and victims of political violence, in particular, should not be underestimated. Forms of approved institutional maltreatment, such as misuse of authority, suggest that reforms are needed. Also, policymakers may have to pay increased attention to the types of programs and policies that should be adopted, such as compensation laws, bills of rights, provision of services, and assistance programs.

RESEARCH IMPLICATIONS

Taking a wider view of the many specific points raised by the study, the combination of quantitative and qualitative techniques within the research design was very useful. Specifically, within the quantitative analysis framework, the study refocused the issue of the moderating effect of social support and has firmly established the impact of sociopolitical conditions on the psychological system of traumatized individuals. Also, many of the predictors of PTSD and psychological problems were confirmed. However, without the qualitative part, the study would have been less adept at capturing the kind of in-depth contextual detail that focus groups provided. The open-response format of the focus groups allowed family members to express their own feelings and experiences, and to identify many obstacles that impaired their posttrauma recovery. Also, the integration of the two methods in the research design enhanced the quality of the results because they combine controlled and automatic cognitive processes in information processing.

Shiffrin and Schneider (1977) made a distinction between controlled and automatic cognitive processes. Controlled processing is initiated deliberately, such as when one answers closed-ended survey questions, whereas automatic processing is triggered by stimuli and includes encoding processes that occur outside consciousness. Thus, the predetermined issues and categories for responding may not be what structures one's perceptions, reactions, and behavior. Also, self-relevant knowledge and stimuli relevant to our current needs and goals are likely to be encoded automatically (Fiske and Taylor, 1991). By the same token, cognitive psychologists (Fiske and Taylor, 1991; Shaver, 1985; Uleman, 1989) view consciousness as a necessary condition for human understanding and intent. Thus, neither quantitative nor qualitative methods are better or worse than the other; they simply differ. Each has its place in mental health research; each complements and compensates for the limitations of the other. However, since the majority of Palestinian research has been gathered through questionnaires that ask for responses expressed on five-point rating scales or other constrained-response categories, researchers are urged to give special consideration to qualitative methods of research. They are particularly useful for exploratory research when little is known about the phenomenon of interest, for change-oriented research, and for policy research. For example, in Palestine, appropriate channels of communication between the Palestinian people and those who hold positions of power are not available, and when frustration is excessive, focus group interaction is useful because it allows groups of people to express their perspectives.

Mental health professionals in Palestine need to gain feedback from traumatized individuals to identify the problems that they encounter and to set the standards for culturally sensitive models of assessment, prevention, and intervention as well as laws and legislation. Specific considerations in research should be given to sociocultural norms, the values, attitudes, and beliefs of Palestinian society in public policymaking and intervention programs. When the affected family members speak out, they provide adequate information about their needs, legal rights for social welfare, health care, and delivery of services.

Despite the new and rediscovered knowledge about the impact of political violence on family members' mental health, many questions remain. To what degree can Western psychological interventions be effective with Palestinians? What aspects of the Palestinian culture buffer the effects of traumatic stress on psychiatric illness? Should support resources focus primarily on financial support and compensation payments, or on emotional support? What are the social and cultural processes within the Palestinian culture that may regulate emotions and create self-help opportunities? Of particular significance are issues of ideology; religiosity; family support, as opposed to political and/or religious group support; objective living standards versus relative group deprivation; experiences of injustices; and posttrauma recovery.

CLOSING REMARKS

Political violence is a predominant contributing factor in the development of mental health problems among Palestinians, most commonly post-traumatic stress disorder. Although post-traumatic reactions arise as a direct result of the experience of political traumas among afflicted family members, the chronicity and severity of reactions are also a function of other psychosocial factors. In particular, the support received from others; the person's appraisal of his or her social, economic, and political condition; and the life events experienced in the posttrauma environment may all exacerbate symptoms. Therefore, I believe that the high prevalence of post-traumatic stress disorder and other co-morbid disorders, such as depression and anxiety, indicate that the traumatic experiences of the affected family members have not been assimilated.

Thus far, the results and analyses contained in this book derive their greatest value when they are viewed as aiding the realization of the goals of treatment, initiation of a mental health policy for victims of political violence, and protection of Palestinian human rights, as reflected in forthcoming legislation and laws. To that end, this book is dedicated.

Appendix A

Factor Structure with Loadings for the Psychiatric Symptoms Index Obtained by Ilfeld and Pilot Study (N = 150)

During the past week, how often did you: (response categories: "never," "once in a while," "fairly often," and "very often")	Factor Loadings	
	Ilfeld	Pilot Study
1. Have trouble remembering things?	.66	.70
2. Have trouble concentrating?	.71	.70
3. Have difficulty making decisions?	.60	.53
4. Have your mind go blank?	.61	.47
5. Have an upset or sour stomach?	.45	.49
6. Have tightness or tension in your neck, back, or other muscles?	.47	.59
7. Feel faint or dizzy?	.59	.63
8. Sweat when not working hard or overheated?	.51	.50
9. Notice your hands trembling?	.58	.47
10. Have to avoid certain things, places, activities because they frighten you?	.39	.34
11. Have your heart pound or race when not physically active?	.55	.42

12. Feel nervous or shaky inside?	.58	.45
13. Have trouble catching your breath?	.53	.54
14. Feel tense or keyed up?	.51	.56
15. Feel fearful or afraid?	.48	.48
16. Have a poor appetite?	.38	.35
17. Feel lonely?	.65	.69
18. Feel bored or have little interest in things?	.59	.73
19. Lose sexual interest or pleasure?	.49	.47
20. Have trouble getting to sleep or staying asleep?	.43	.55
21. Cry easily or feel like crying?	.54	.57
22. Feel downhearted or blue?	.70	.68
23. Feel low in energy or slowed down?	.47	.47
24. Feel hopeless about the future?	.60	.51
25. Have any thoughts about possibly ending your life?	.30	.71
26. Lose your temper?	.61	.56
27. Feel easily annoyed or irritated?	.76	.67
28. Feel critical of others?	.60	.62
29. Get angry over things that are not too important?	.70	.73

The four factors obtained by Ilfeld (1976) represent a distinct and definable cluster of symptoms. Factor 1, items 5 through 15, describes a rather typical syndrome of anxiety. Factor 2, items 26 through 29, reflects anger. Factor 3, items 16 through 25, captures a syndrome of depression. Factor 4, items 1 through 4, delineates cognitive disturbance.

Appendix B

Factor Structure with Loadings
for the Well-Being Scale (N = 150)

Item Number	Item Description	Factor Loadings

During the past month, I felt:

Factor 1: Happiness and Peacefulness

2.	Cheerful	.85
3.	Delighted	.81
1.	Happy	.78
4.	Relaxed	.72
6.	Safe	.58
5.	Calm and peaceful	.57

Factor 2: Vigorousness

8.	Responsive	.81
7.	Active	.80
9.	Healthy	.71

Appendix C

Factor Structure with Loadings for the Trauma-Induced Stress Scale (N = 150)

Item Number	Item Description	Factor Loadings

Did the catastrophe have a negative impact on:

Factor 1: Strains in Work and Family

3.	Your financial status?	.82
1.	Your physical health?	.72
8.	Your management of family affairs?	.62
4.	Your work?	.61
7.	Your family growth?	.59
11.	Your life in general?	.59
6.	Your social activities?	.59

Factor 2: Strains in Family Relationships

10.	Your family's relationship with relatives?	.81
9.	Your relationship with your family members?	.78

Factor 3: Strains in Marriage and Health

2.	Your mental health?	.77
5.	Your marriage?	.65

Appendix D

Factor Structure with Loadings for the Role Strains Scale (N = 150)

Item Number	Item Description	Factor Loadings
	Factor 1: Role Demands Regarding Family's Supply and Care	
7. The difficulty in paying my debts has increased.		.70
12. My responsibility to provide money for the family has increased.		.64
4. The tasks that I should accomplish have increased.		.55
1. My difficulties in handling children's matters have increased.		.55
8. My responsibility in providing direct care for some family members has increased.		.54
3. The problems and issues that need to be solved have increased.		.51
	Factor 2: Role Strains Regarding the Absence of Spouse	
13. My responsibility in providing direct care for a family member who has become physically handicapped or sick has increased.		.67

2. The length of time my spouse is away
   from home has increased.   .63
9. Disputes with relatives because of their
   interference in my life have increased.   .61
18. Understanding my spouse has become difficult.   .52

Factor 3: Interrole Conflict

5. The difficulty in compromising between my
   family role and my working role has increased.   .66
10. My responsibility at work has increased.   .64
6. My activities outside the home have increased.   .63
11. My difficulty in providing adequate care for
    the children while at work has increased.   .63

Factor 4: Role Obligations

15. My responsibility in meeting my children's
    emotional needs has increased.   .76
19. My role has become more demanding.   .56
17. My home chore load has increased.   .47
14. My responsibility in helping my children
    with their schoolwork has increased.   .46

Factor 5: Role Strain in Satisfying Spousal Needs

16. My responsibility in meeting spousal needs
    has increased.   .71

Appendix E

Factor Structure with Loadings for the Ideology Scale (N = 150)

Item Number	Item Description	Factor Loadings
	Factor 1: Attitudes Toward Political Party	
6.	The person who gets involved with political parties opposed to mine loses people's trust.	.79
7.	We should not have trust in other political parties.	.78
9.	Sometimes I wonder how a person allows himself/herself to be affiliated with a political party different from mine.	.74
8.	Opposing political parties have the right to compete with our political party in all fields and activities.	.58
11.	Most citizens are exploited by political parties other than their own.	.48
	Factor 2: Commitment to Religion As Faith and Practice	
2.	Religious commitment solves our problems.	.85
1.	Religious commitment reduces our problems.	.85

5. The *sharia* (Islamic Law) should be the main source
   of the laws of the state.   .77

Factor 3: Commitment to Political-Religious Principles and Practices

10. The person who refuses to trade his or her
    political beliefs for personal benefit should
    be rewarded.   .75

4. The person who refuses to trade his or her
   religious beliefs for personal benefit should
   be rewarded.   .70

3. The person who refuses holy war is not a
   good person.   .65

Appendix F

Factor Structure with Loadings for the Social Support Scale (N = 150)

Item Number	Item Description	Factor Loadings
	Factor 1: Support Received from Significant Others	
6.	My family members keep me company when I need them.	.90
7.	My relatives provide me with advice when I need it.	.90
11.	My friends are always ready to listen to my problems.	.89
10.	I am contented with my friends around me.	.89
5.	The relationship among my family members is characterized by emotional support.	.89
9.	I don't have a close relationship with my relatives.	.88
4.	My family assists me financially when it is necessary.	.87
8.	My relatives encourage me to overcome the difficulties that I face.	.81

12. My friends come to me only when they need me. .81

17. I get help from institutions that provide counseling. .71

16. I find difficulty in finding professional help. .64

 3. My family encourages me to overcome
the difficulties that I face. .64

 2. My family gives me advice when I need it. .64

Factor 2: Provision and Receipt of Social Support
from Social Institutions

19. There are institutions and programs in our
community that help families who have problems
like ours. .86

18. There are social institutions in our community
that offer help (financial and moral). .82

20. One of the private institutions provides me
with financial assistance. .80

21. I find great difficulty in getting help from
the social institutions that offer help to families
who have problems like ours. .65

 1. My family does not support me when I am in need. .53

Factor 3: Religious Group Support

25. My religious group helps me to solve my problems. .98

24. Members of my religious group help me to solve
my problems. .98

22. My religious group provides me with adequate
moral support. .97

23. My religious group provides me with the financial
support to meet my needs. .96

Factor 4: Political Group Support

15. My political group provides me with financial
    support when I am in need.   .96
13. My political group refers to me only when
    they need me.   .96
14. My political group provides me with the moral
    support that I need.   .95

Appendix G

Factor Structure with Loadings for the Coping Scale (N = 150)

Item Number	Item Description	Factor Loadings

When I am confronted with problems and difficulties:

Factor 1: Problem-Focused Coping

29.	I say maybe it is better for me the way things are.	.78
24.	I look to my relatives.	.76
8.	I participate in religious activities.	.76
28.	I look at my problem positively.	.76
2.	I seek information and advice from professionals.	.76
6.	I seek social support from friends.	.74
1.	I seek information and advice from religious people.	.74
27.	I believe that what has happened to me is my fate.	.66
7.	I pray.	.66
3.	I seek help from local institutions and programs that are established to help.	.65
16.	I seek information and advice from my relatives.	.59
21.	I depend on one of the institutions for my expenditures.	.55
4.	I seek information and advice from the family doctor.	.43

Factor 2: Emotion-Focused Coping

22. I seek social support from my family.	.75
26. I accept the difficulties that have occurred to me.	.71
25. I am restricted by problems in a way that I withhold my immediate actions.	.71
20. I depend on myself in solving family matters.	.70
18. I express my feelings through anger.	.70
5. I seek social support from my relatives.	.66
17. I cry.	.63
30. I look at the positive things that I have in order to be grateful for having them.	.57

Factor 3: Seeking Support from Significant Others

13. I seek financial support from my family.	.77
14. I seek information and advice from my family.	.76
15. I seek moral support from my family.	.75
23. I look to my friends.	.50

Factor 4: Seeking Support from Political and Religious Groups

11. I seek information and advice from my political party.	.96
10. I ask help from members of my political party.	.96
9. I seek help from my political party.	.94
12. I seek help from my religious group.	.59

Factor 5: Autonomy and Independence
in Dealing with Problematic Situations

32. I depend on myself in solving problems.	.88
31. I depend on myself in making decisions.	.88
33. I draw on my past experience in solving problems.	.57
19. I depend on myself in solving financial matters.	.50

Appendix H

Factor Structure with Loadings for the Sociopolitical Satisfaction Scale (N = 150)

Item Number	Item Description	Factor Loadings

During the past four weeks, how satisfied were you:

Factor 1: Satisfaction with the Political Situation

11.	With the accomplishments of the peace treaty?	.81
9.	With the current political situation?	.79
10.	With political progress?	.76
12.	With the amount of political security that is provided for you and your family?	.74
13.	With your life in general?	.52

Factor 2: Satisfaction with Work

5.	With the salary and benefits you get for your work?	.81
7.	With the amount of security for the future of your family that you get in your job?	.79

6. With the personal growth that you get
in your work?   .78

8. With the feelings of worth that you get
from your job?   .67

4. With the amount of security at your work?   .52

Factor 3: Satisfaction with Social Life

3. With your social relationships?   .79

2. With the amount of happiness in your social life?   .68

1. With the social security that you have?   .55

Appendix I

Guide for Focus Group Discussions

Introductory Questions

State your name and the trauma that was encountered (e.g., a family member killed, imprisoned, injured, house demolished).

1. What are the most serious problems facing your family since the trauma?

2. A number of concerns have been mentioned. Think about families who live in armed conflict. How do their problems compare to those already mentioned?

3. In your community, what are the resources that you draw on for help?

4. Do you have anyone that you feel you can talk to about what you have been through?

5. How have your friends and your family responded to you since the traumatic event?

6. Tell us about the circumstances under which you seek help. When and where is help most likely to be given?

7. How well do you feel you have coped since the trauma?

8. Let's talk about what can be done to help families cope with trauma. Let's start with the Palestinian National Authority (PNA):

a. What do you think the PNA could do that would help families cope with trauma?

b. What are the best ways for families to communicate with the PNA about their problems and other concerns and issues?

c. What about community organizations? What can they do to help people cope?

d. Who are the other groups or individuals that might be of help in meeting your needs, and what could they do?

(After they have answered, hand out the list of groups.)

This is a list of some of the groups that might give some help. As I read through the list, please feel free to comment on what you think any of these groups might be able to do:

- Professional helpers (e.g., counselors)
- Charitable organizations
- Social welfare department—local community
- Religious leaders
- Religious groups
- Political parties
- Employers
- Other

9. What are the things in our lives that could make it easier for us to be healthy, happy, and independent in the future?

(After they have answered, hand out the list of activities.)

In addition, how could the following things influence you?

Activities

- Social
- Sports
- Music
- Hobbies
- Mosque (Church)
- Other

Community Service Opportunities

- Job opportunities
- Supportive family
- Spiritual or religious beliefs
- Educational and/or vocational goals

10. Are there any of these you would like to see more of in your community?

11. Let's summarize the key points of our discussion. (The assistant moderator will give a brief two-minute summary of the responses to questions 6, 7, and 8.) Does this summary sound complete? Do you have any changes or additions to make?

12. The goal is to help families suffering from political violence cope. Have we missed anything?

13. What advice do you have for us?

References

Aldwin, C. and Revenson, T. (1987). Does coping help? An examination of the relation between coping and mental health. *Journal of Personality and Social Psychology, 53,* 237-248.

Allodi, F. (1980). The psychiatric effects in children and families of victims of political persecution and torture. *Danish Medical Bulletin, 27,* 229-332.

Allodi, F. and Cowgill, G. (1982). Ethical and psychiatric aspects of torture. *Canadian Journal of Psychiatry, 27,* 98-102.

American Psychiatric Association (1994). *Diagnostic and statistical manual of mental disorders* (Fourth edition). Washington, DC: American Psychiatric Association.

Andrews, F. and Robinson, J. (1991). Measures of subjective well-being. In P. Robinson, P.R. Shaver, and L.S. Wrightsman (Eds.), *Measures of personality and social psychological attitudes* (pp. 61-114). San Diego, CA: Academic Press.

Andrews, F. and Withey, S. (1976). *Social indicators of well-being: Americans' perceptions of life quality.* New York: Plenum Press.

Antonovsky, A. (1979). *Health, stress and coping.* San Francisco: Jossey-Bass.

Badri, M.B. (1979). *The dilemma of Muslim psychologists.* London: MWH Publishers.

Bailey, B., Hallinan, M., Contreras, R., and Hernandez, A.G. (1985). Disaster response: The need for community mental health center preparedness. *Journal of Mental Health Administration, 12,* 42-46.

Bakan, D. (1968). *Disease, pain and sacrifice: Toward a psychology of suffering.* Chicago: University of Chicago Press.

Baker, A. and Kevorkian, N. (1995). Differential effects of trauma on spouses of traumatized households. *Journal of Traumatic Stress, 8,* 61-74.

Bardo, J. (1976). Dimensions of community satisfaction in a British new town. *Multivariate Experimental Clinical Research, 2,* 129-134.

Beck, A., Emery, G., and Greenberg, R. (1985). *Anxiety disorders and phobias: A cognitive perspective.* New York: Basic Books.

Berenbaum, H., Fujita, F., and Pfennig, J. (1995). Consistency, specificity, and correlates of negative emotions. *Journal of Personality and Social Psychology, 68,* 342-352.

Bergman, L. and Magnusson, D. (1979). Over-achievement and catecholamine excretion in an achievement-demanding situation. *Psychosomatic Medicine, 41,* 181-188.

Billings, A. and Moos, R. (1981). The role of coping responses and social resources in attenuating the stress of life events. *Journal of Behavioral Medicine, 4,* 139-157.

Billings, A. and Moos, R. (1984). Coping, stress, and social resources among adults with unipolar depression. *Journal of Personality and Social Psychology, 46,* 877-891.

Blake, D., Albano, A., and Keane, T. (1992). Twenty years of trauma: Psychological abstracts 1970 through 1989. *Journal of Traumatic Stress, 5,* 477-484.

Bonan, B. and Eduards, M. (1984). The Indochinese refugees: An overview. *Australian and New Zealand Journal of Psychiatry, 18,* 40-52.

Boss, P.G. (1988). *Family stress management.* Newbury Park, CA: Sage.

Brown, G.W. and Harris, T. (1978). *Social origins of depression: A study of psychiatric disorder in women.* New York: Free Press.

Campbell, A., Converse, P.E., and Rodgers, W.L. (1976). *The quality of American life.* New York: Russell Sage Foundation.

Casella, L. and Motta, R.W. (1995). The effect of PTSD and combat level on Vietnam veterans' perceptions of child behavior and marital adjustment. *Journal of Clinical Psychology, 51,* 4-12.

Cohen, J. (1985). Trauma and repression. *Psychoanalytic Inquiry, 5,* 164-189.

Cohen, S. and Hoberman, G. (1983). Positive events and social support and buffers of life change stress. *Journal of Applied Social Psychology, 13,* 423-439.

Cohen, S. and Wills, T. (1985). Stress, social support, and the buffering hypothesis. *Psychological Bulletin, 98,* 310-357.

Cormie, K. and Howell, J.M. (1988). A mental health component in the public health response to disasters. *Canadian Journal of Public Health, 79,* 97-100.

Costa, P.T., Jr., and McCrae, R.R. (1980). Influence of extroversion and neuroticism on subjective well-being: Happy and unhappy people. *Journal of Personality and Social Psychology, 38,* 668-678.

Cutrona, C. (1989). Ratings of social support by adolescents and adult informants: Degree of correspondence and prediction of depressive symptoms. *Journal of Personality and Social Psychology, 57,* 723-730.

Davis, E.E., Fine-Davis, M., and Meehan, G. (1982). Demographic determinants of perceived well-being in eight European countries. *Social Indicator Research, 10,* 341-350.

Dean, A. and Lin, N. (1977). The stress-buffering role of social support. *Journal of Nervous and Mental Disease, 165,* 403-417.

Defazio, V.J. and Pascucci, N.J. (1984). Return to Ithaca: A perspective on marriage and love in posttraumatic stress disorder. *Journal of Contemporary Psychotherapy, 14,* 76-89.

Denzin, N. (1970). *The research act: A theoretical introduction to sociological methods.* Chicago: Aldine.

Diener, E. and Diener, M. (1995). Cross-cultural correlates of life satisfaction and self-esteem. *Journal of Personality and Social Psychology, 68,* 653-663.

Diener, E. and Larsen, R.J. (1993). The experience of emotional well-being. In M. Lewis and J.M. Haviland (Eds.), *Handbook of emotions* (pp. 405-415). New York: Guilford Press.

Diwan, I. and Radwan, S. (1999). *Development under adversity. The Palestinian economy in transition.* Ramallah: Palestine Economic Policy Research Institute and World Bank.

Dohrenwend, B.S. and Dohrenwend, B.P. (Eds.) (1974). *Stressful events: Their nature and effects.* New York: Wiley.

Elliot, G.R. and Eisdorfer, C. (1982). *Stress and human health.* New York: Springer.

Emmons, R.A. (1986). Personal strivings: An approach to personality and subjective well-being. *Journal of Personality and Social Psychology, 51,* 1058-1068.

Emmons, R.A. and Diener, E. (1985). Personality correlates of subjective well-being. *Personality and Social Psychology Bulletin, 11,* 89-97.

Eranen, L. and Liebkind, K. (1993). Coping with disaster: The helping behavior of communities and individuals. In J. Wilson and B. Raphael (Eds.), *International handbook of traumatic stress syndromes* (pp. 957-964). New York: Plenum Press.

Fairley, M. (1984). *Tropical cyclone Oscar: Psychological reactions of a Fijian population.* Paper presented at the Disaster Research Workshop, Mt. Macedon, Victoria, Australia.

Fiore, J., Becker, J., and Coppel, D. (1983). Social network interactions: A buffer or a stress? *American Journal of Community Psychology, 11,* 423-439.

Fiore, N. (1979). Fighting cancer: One patient's perspective. *New England Journal of Medicine, 300,* 284-289.

Fiske, S. and Taylor, S. (1991). *Social cognition.* New York: McGraw-Hill.

Folkman, S. and Lazarus, R. (1980). An analysis of coping in a middle-aged community sample. *Journal of Health and Social Behavior, 21,* 219-239.

Folkman, S. and Lazarus, R. (1985). If it changes it must be a process: A study of emotions and coping during three stages of a college examination. *Journal of Personality and Social Psychology, 48,* 150-170.

Folkman, S., Lazarus, R., Gruen, R., and Delongis, A. (1986). Appraisal, coping, health status, and psychological symptoms. *Journal of Personality and Social Psychology, 50,* 557-579.

Fredrick, C. (1985). Children traumatized by catastrophic situations. In S. Eth and R. Pynoos (Eds.), *Post-traumatic stress disorder in children* (pp. 71-100). Washington, DC: American Psychiatric Press.

Freedy, J. and Donkervoet, J. (1995). Traumatic stress: An overview of the field. In J. Freedy and S. Hobfoll (Eds.), *Traumatic stress: From theory to practice* (pp. 3-28). New York: Plenum Press.

Gleser, G.C., Green, B.L., and Winget, C.N. (1981). *Prolonged psychosocial effects of disaster: A study of Buffalo Greek.* New York: Academic Press.

Goldfeld, A.E., Mollica, R.F., Pesavento, B.H., and Faraone, S.V. (1988). The physical and psychological sequelae of torture: Symptomatology and diagnosis. *Journal of the American Medical Association, 259,* 2725-2729.

Goode, W. (1960). A theory of role strain. *American Sociological Review, 25,* 483-496.

Goudy, W. (1977). Evaluations of local attributes and community satisfaction in small towns. *Rural Sociology, 42,* 371-382.

Green, B. (1993). Identifying survivors at risk: Trauma and stressors across events. In J. Wilson and B. Raphael (Eds.), *International handbook of traumatics stress syndromes* (pp. 135-144). New York: Plenum Press.

Green, B.L. and Grace, M.C. (1988). Conceptual issues in research with survivors and illustrations from a follow-up study. In J.P. Wilson, Z. Harel, and B. Kahana (Eds.), *Human adaptation to extreme stress: From the Holocaust to Vietnam* (pp. 105-124). New York: Plenum Press.

Green, B. and Solomon, S. (1995). The mental health impact of natural and technological disasters, In J. Freedy and S.E. Hobfoll (Eds.), *Traumatic stress: From theory to practice* (pp. 163-180). New York: Plenum Press.

Hadden, D. and McDevitt, D. (1974). Environmental stress and thyrotoxicosis. *Lancet, 11*, 577.

Hann, N. (1977). *Coping and defending: Processes of self-environment organization.* New York: Academic Press.

Hines, A.M. (1993). Linking qualitative and quantitative methods in cross-cultural survey research: Techniques from cognitive science. *American Journal of Community Psychology, 21*, 729-746.

Hirsch, B. and Rapkin, B. (1986). Multiple roles, social networks, and women's well-being. *Journal of Personality and Social Psychology, 51*, 1237-1247.

Hobfoll, S., Dunahoo, C., and Monnier, J. (1995). Conservation of resources and traumatic stress. In J.R. Freedy and S.E. Hobfoll (Eds.), *Traumatic stress: From theory to practice.* New York: Plenum Press.

Holahan, C. and Moos, R. (1987). Personal and contextual determinants of coping strategies. *Journal of Personality and Social Psychology, 52*, 946-955.

Holahan, C. and Moos, R. (1990). Life stressors, resistance factors, and psychological health: An extension of the stress-resistance paradigm. *Journal of Personality and Social Psychology, 58*, 909- 917.

Holahan, C. and Moos, R. (1991). Life stressors, personal and social resources and depression: A 4-year structural model. *Journal of Abnormal Psychology, 100*, 31-38.

Hosmer, D.W., Jr., and Lemeshow, S. (1989). *Applied logistic regression.* New York: Wiley.

Hughes, D., Seidman, E., and Williams, N. (1993). Cultural phenomena and the research enterprise: Toward a culturally anchored methodology. *American Journal of Community Psychology, 21*, 687-703.

Ilfeld, F. (1976). Further validation of psychiatric symptom index in a normal population. *Psychological Report, 39*, 1213-1228.

Joseph, S., Williams, R., and Yule, W. (1997). *Understanding post-traumatic stress: A psychological perspective on PTSD and treatment.* New York: Wiley.

Jurich, A.P. (1983). The Saigon of the family's mind: Family therapy with families of Vietnam veterans. *Journal of Marital and Family Therapy, 9*, 355-363.

Kahana, E., Midlarsky, E., and Kahana, B. (1987). Beyond dependency, autonomy and exchange: Prosocial behavior in late life adaptation. *Social Justice Research, 1*, 439-459.

Kessler, M. and Albee, G. (1975). Primary prevention. *Annual Review of Psychology, 26,* 557-591.

Kessler, R. and Mcleod, J. (1985). Social support and mental health in community samples. In S. Cohen and S.L. Syme (Eds.), *Social support and health* (pp. 219-240). San Diego, CA: Academic Press.

Khamis, V. (1993a). Posttraumatic stress disorder among the injured of the *intifada*. *Journal of Traumatic Stress, 6,* 555-559.

Khamis, V. (1993b). Victims of the *intifada:* The psychosocial adjustment of the injured. *Behavioral Medicine, 19,* 93-101.

Khamis, V. (1995a). Coping with stress: Palestinian families and *intifada*-related trauma. Unpublished manuscript. Palestine: Bethlehem University.

Khamis, V. (1995b). Psychological sequelae of *intifada*-related trauma in Palestinian families. Unpublished manuscript. Palestine: Bethlehem University.

Khamis, V. (1998). Psychological distress and well-being among traumatized Palestinian women during the *intifada. Social Science and Medicine, 46,* 1033-1041.

Kinzie, J.D. (1989). Therapeutic approaches to traumatized Cambodian refugees. *Journal of Traumatic Stress, 2,* 185-198.

Kleinbaum, D.G., Kupper, L.L., and Morgenstern, H. (1982). *Epidemiologic research: Principles and quantitative methods.* New York: Van Nostrand Reinhold.

Knodel, J. (1993). The design and analysis of focus group studies: A practical approach. In D. Morgan (Ed.), *Successful focus groups: Advancing the state of the art* (pp. 35-50). Newbury Park, CA: Sage.

Kobasa, S. (1979). Stressful life events, personality and health: An inquiry into hardiness. *Journal of Personality and Social Psychology, 37,* 1-11.

Krueger, R. (1994). *Focus groups: A practical guide for applied research* (Second edition). Beverly Hills, CA: Sage.

Lakey, B. and Lutz, C. (1996). Social support and preventive and therapeutic interventions. In G. Pierce, B. Sarason, and I. Sarason (Eds.), *Handbook of social support and the family* (pp. 435-465). New York: Plenum Press.

Lazarus, R. (1966). *Psychological stress and the coping process.* New York: McGraw-Hill.

Lazarus, R. (1981). The stress and coping paradigm. In C. Eisdorfer, D. Cohen, A. Kleinman, and P. Maxim (Eds.), *Models in clinical psychopathology* (pp. 117-214). New York: Spectrum.

Lazarus, R. and Folkman, S. (1984). *Stress, appraisal, and coping.* New York: Springer.

Lima, B.R., Chavez, H., Samaniego, N., Pomei, M.S., Pai, S., Santacruz, H., and Lozano, J. (1989). Disaster severity and emotional disturbance: Implications for primary mental health care in developing countries. *Acta Psychiatrica Scandinavica, 79,* 74-82.

Lima, B.R., Pai, S., Santacruz, H., Lozano, J., and Luna, J. (1987). Screening for the psychological consequences of a major disaster in a developing country: Armero, Colombia. *Acta Psychiatrica Scandinavica, 76,* 561-567.

Long, J. and Porter, K. (1984). Multiple roles of midlife women: A case for new directions in theory, research, and policy. In G. Baruch and J. Brooks-Gunn (Eds.), *Between youth and old age: Women in the middle years* (pp. 109-160). New York: Plenum Press.

Lopez-Ibor, J.J., Jr., Canas, S.F., and Rodriguez-Gamazo, M. (1985). Psychological aspects of the toxic oil syndrome catastrophe. *British Journal of Psychiatry, 147,* 352-365.

Lyons, J.A. and Keane, T.M. (1989). Implosive therapy for the treatment of combat-related PTSD. *Journal of Traumatic Stress, 2,* 93-111.

Madakasira, S. and O'Brien, K.F. (1987). Acute posttraumatic stress disorder in victims of natural disaster. *Journal of Nervous and Mental Disease, 175,* 286-290.

Magnusson, D. (1982). Situational determinants of stress: An interactional perspective. In L. Goldberger and S. Breznitz (Eds.), *Handbook of stress: Theoretical and clinical aspects* (pp. 231-253). New York: Free Press.

Maloney, L.J. (1988). Posttraumatic stress disorder on women partners of Vietnam veterans. *Smith College Studies in Social Work, 58,* 122-143.

Marans, R. and Rodgers, W. (1975). Toward an understanding of community satisfaction. In A.H. Hawley and V.P. Rock (Eds.), *Metropolitan America in contemporary perspective* (pp. 299-352). New York: Wiley.

Marks, S. (1977). Multiple roles and role strain: Some notes on human energy, time and commitment. *American Sociological Review, 42,* 921-936.

Palestinian Economic Policy Research Institute (MAS) (1998a). *Economic monitor* (issue no. 3). Jerusalem: Palestinian Economic Policy Research Institute.

Palestinian Economic Policy Research Institute (MAS) (1998b). *Social monitor* (issue no. 1). Jerusalem: Palestinian Economic Policy Research Institute.

Maton, K.I. (1993). A bridge between cultures: Linked ethnographic-empirical methodology for culture-anchored research. *American Journal of Community Psychology, 21,* 747-773.

McCrae, R.R. (1982). Age differences in the use of coping mechanisms. *Journal of Gerontology, 37,* 454-460.

McCubbin, H.I. and Patterson, J. (1983). Family stress adaptation to crisis: A double ABCX model of behavior. In H. McCubbin, M. Sussman, and J. Patterson (Eds.), *Social stresses and the family: Advances and developments in family stress theory and research* (pp. 7-37). Binghamton, NY: The Haworth Press, Inc.

McFarlane, A.C. (1986). Posttraumatic morbidity of a disaster: A study of cases presented for psychiatric treatment. *Journal of Nervous and Mental Disease, 17,* 4-13.

McFarlane, A.C. (1988). The etiology of posttraumatic stress disorders following a natural disaster. *British Journal of Psychiatry, 152,* 116-121.

McKenry, P. and Price, S. (1994). Families coping with problems and change. In P. McKenry and S. Price (Eds.), *Families and change: Coping with stressful events* (pp. 1-18). Thousand Oaks, CA: Sage Publications.

Menaghan, E.G. (1983). Individual coping efforts and family studies: Conceptual and methodological issues. *Marriage and Family Review, 6,* 113-135.

Merton, R. (1968). *Social theory and social structure* (Revised edition). New York: Free Press.

Michalos, A.C. (1980). Satisfaction and happiness. *Social Indicators Research, 8,* 385-422.

Michalos, A.C. (1983). Satisfaction and happiness in a rural northern resource community. *Social Indicators Research, 13,* 225-252.

Michalos, A.C. (1985). Multiple discrepancies theory (MDT). *Social Indicators Research, 16,* 347-414.

Mitchell, R.E. and Hodson, C.A. (1986). Coping and social support among battered women: An ecological perspective. In S. Hobfoll (Ed.), *Stress, social support and women* (pp. 152-153). Washington, DC: Hemisphere Publishing.

Morgan, D. (1988). *Focus groups as qualitative research.* Newbury Park, CA: Sage Publication.

Motta, R.W. (1990). Personal and interfamilial effects of the Vietnam war experience. *Behavior Therapist, 13,* 155-157.

Myers, D. and Diener, E. (1995). Who is happy? *Psychological Science, 6,* 10-19.

Nixon, A. (1990). *The status of Palestinian children during the uprising in the occupied territories.* East Jerusalem: Swedish Save the Children.

Norris, F. and Thompson, M. (1995). Applying community psychology to the prevention of trauma and traumatic life events. In J. Freedy and S. Hobfoll (Eds.), *Traumatic stress: From theory to practice* (pp. 49-72). New York: Plenum Press.

Norusis, M. (1992). *SPSS-PC+[tm], version 5.0.* Chicago: SPSS Inc.

Ortony, A., Clore, G.L., and Collins, A. (1988). *The cognitive structure of emotions.* Cambridge, England: Cambridge University Press.

Pagel, M., Erdly, W., and Becker, J. (1987). Social networks: We get by with (and in spite of) a little help from our friends. *Journal of Personality and Social Psychology, 53,* 793-804.

Paker, M., Paker, O., and Yüksel, S. (1992). Psychological effects of torture: An empirical study of tortured and non-tortured non-political prisoners. In M. Basoglu (Ed.), *Torture and its consequences* (pp. 72-82). New York: Cambridge University Press.

Parkes, W. (1977). Stress factors in Northern Ireland as seen from a coronary care unit. *Practitioner, 218,* 409-416.

Parsons, T. (1957). Motivation of religious beliefs and behavior. In J. M. Yinger (Ed.), *Religion, society and the individual* (pp. 380-385). New York: Macmillan.

Pearlin, L. (1983). Role strains and personal stress. In H. Kaplan (Ed.), *Psychosocial stress: Trends in theory and research* (pp. 3-32). New York: Academic Press.

Pearlin, L. (1989). The sociological study of stress. *Journal of Health and Social Behavior, 30,* 241-256.

Pearlin, L. (1993). The social contexts of stress. In L. Goldberger and S. Breznitz (Eds.), *Handbook of stress: Theoretical and clinical aspects* (pp. 303-315). New York: Free Press.

Pearlin, L. and Lieberman, M. (1979). Social sources of emotional distress. In R. Simmons (Ed.), *Research in community and mental health* (pp. 217-248) (Volume 1). Greenwich, CT: JAI Press.

Pearlin, L., Lieberman, M., Menagham, E., and Mullin, J. (1981). The stress process. *Journal of Health and Social Behavior, 22,* 337-356.

Pearlin, L. and Schooler, C. (1978). The structure of coping. *Journal of Health and Social Behavior, 19,* 2-21.

Perry, R. and Lindell, M. (1978). The psychological consequences of natural disaster: A review of research on American communities. *Mass Emergencies, 3,* 105-115.

Pierce, G., Sarason, B., Sarason, I., Joseph, H., and Henderson, C. (1996). Conceptualizing and assessing social support in the context of the family. In G. Pierce, B. Sarason, and I. Sarason (Eds.), *Handbook of social support and the family* (pp. 3-23). New York: Plenum Press.

Raphael, B. and Wilson, J. (1993). Theoretical and intervention considerations in working with victims of disaster. In J. Wilson and B. Raphael (Eds.), *International handbook of traumatic stress syndromes* (pp. 105-117). New York: Plenum Press.

Rasmussen, O.V. and Lunde, I. (1980). Evaluation of investigation of 200 torture victims. *Danish Medical Bulletin, 27,* 241-243.

Resick, P.A. (1992). Cognitive treatment of crime-related post-traumatic stress disorder. In R.J. McMahon and V.L. Quinsey (Eds.), *Aggression and violence throughout the life span* (pp. 171-191). Newbury Park, CA: Sage Publications.

Richardson, S., Dohrenwend, B., and Klein, D. (1965). *Interviewing: Its forms and functions.* New York: Basic Books.

Rigamer, J. (1986). Psychological management of children in a national crisis. *Journal of the American Academy of Child Psychiatry, 25,* 364-369.

Rojek, D., Clemente, F., and Summers, G. (1975). Community satisfaction: A study of contentment with local services. *Rural Sociology, 40,* 177-192.

Rook, K.S. (1984). The negative side of social interaction: Impact on psychological well-being. *Journal of Personality and Social Psychology, 46,* 1097-1108.

Roseman, I.J. (1991). Appraisal determinants of discrete emotions. *Cognition and Emotion, 5,* 161-200.

Rosenhech, R. and Thompson, J. (1986). "Detoxication" of Vietnam war trauma: A combined family-individual approach. *Family Process, 25,* 559-570.

Rothbaum, B.O. and Foa, E.B. (1992). Cognitive-behavioral treatment of post-traumatic stress disorder. In P.A. Saigh (Ed.), *Posttraumatic stress disorder: A behavioral approach to assesssment and treatment* (pp. 85-110). New York: Pergamon Press.

Sarason, B., Sarason, I., Hacker, T., and Basham, R. (1985). Concomitants of social support: Social skills, physical attractiveness, and gender. *Journal of Personality and Social Psychology, 49,* 469-480.

Sarraj, E., Punamaki, R., Salmi, S., and Summerfield, D. (1996). Experiences of torture and ill-treatment and posttraumatic stress disorder symptoms among Palestinian political prisoners. *Journal of Traumatic Stress, 9,* 595-606.

Scott, M., and Stradling, S. (1993). *Counseling for posttraumatic stress disorder.* London: Sage Publications.

Seltiz, C., Jahoda, M., Deutsch, M., and Cook, S. (1965). *Research methods in social relations.* New York: Holt, Rinehart and Winston.

Shalev, A. (1996). Stress versus traumatic stress: From acute homeostatic reactions to chronic psychopathology. In B.A. van der Kolk, A.C. McFarlane, and L. Weisaeth (Eds.), *Traumatic stress: The effects of overwhelming experience on mind, body, and society* (pp. 77-101). New York: The Guilford Press.

Shanan, J., De-Nour, A., and Garty, I. (1976). Effects of prolonged stress on coping style in terminal renal failure patients. *Journal of Human Stress, 4,* 19-27.

Shaver, K. (1985). *The attribution of blame: Causality, responsibility, and blameworthiness.* New York: Springer-Verlag.

Shiffrin, R. and Schneider, W. (1977). Controlled and automatic human information processing, 11. Perceptual learning, automatic attending, and a general theory. *Psychological Review, 84,* 127-190.

Shore, J.H., Tatum, E.L., and Vollmer, W.M. (1986). The Mount St. Helens stress response syndrome. In J.H. Shore (Ed.), *Disaster stress studies: New methods and findings* (pp. 7-97). Washington, DC: American Psychiatric Press.

Sieber, S. (1974). Toward a theory of role accumulation. *American Sociological Review, 39,* 567-578.

Smith, E. and North, C. (1993). Posttraumatic stress disorder in natural disasters and technological accidents. In J. Wilson and B. Raphael (Eds.), *International handbook of traumatic stress syndromes* (pp. 405-419). New York: Plenum Press.

Solomon, Z. (1988). The effect of combat-related posttraumatic stress disorder on the family. *Psychiatry, 51,* 323-329.

Strupp, H.H. and Binder, J.L. (1984). *Psychotherapy in a new key.* New York: Basic Books.

Stryker, S. (1980). *Symbolic interactionism: A social-structural version.* Menlo Park, CA: Benjamin/Cummings.

Symonds, M. (1980). The "second injury" to victims. In L. Kivens (Ed.), *Evaluation and change: Services for survivors* (pp. 36-38). Minneapolis, MN: Minneapolis Medical Research Foundation.

Tamari, S., Kassis., N., and Khamis, V. (1989, August/September). *Rehabilitation program for the handicapped of the intifada.* Jerusalem: YMCA.

Terry, D. (1991). Stress, coping, and adaptation to new parenthood. *Journal of Personal and Social Relationships, 8,* 527-547.

Terry, D. (1994). Determinants of coping: The role of stable and situational factors. *Journal of Personality and Social Psychology, 66,* 895-910.

Thoits, P.A. (1983). Multiple identities and psychological well-being: A reformulation and test of the social isolation hypothesis. *American Sociological Review, 48,* 174-187.

Thoits, P. (1986). Social support as coping assistance. *Journal of Consulting and Clinical Psychology, 54,* 416-423.

Turner, J.C. (1982). Towards a cognitive redefinition of the social group. In H. Tajfel (Ed.), *Social identity and intergroup relations* (pp. 15-40). New York: Cambridge University Press.

Turner, S. and Gorst-Unsworth, C. (1993). Psychological sequelae of torture. In J. Wilson and B. Raphael (Eds.), *International handbook of traumatic stress syndromes* (pp. 703-713). New York: Plenum Press.

Uleman, J.S. (1989). A framework for thinking intentionally about unintended thoughts. In J.S. Uleman and J.A. Bargh (Eds.), *Unintended thought* (pp. 425-449). New York: Guilford Press.

United Nations Conference on Trade and Development (UNCTAD) (1994a). Prospect for sustained development of the Palestinian economy in the West Bank and Gaza Strip, 1990-2010: A quantitative framework. November 11, 1994.

United Nations Conference on Trade and Development (UNCTAD) (1994b). Health conditions and services in the West Bank and Gaza Strip. September 28, 1994.

United Nations Disaster Relief Co-ordinator (UNDRO) (1986). *Disaster prevention and mitigation:* Volumes 11 and 12, *Preparedness and social aspects.* New York: United Nations.

Vanfossen, B. (1986). Sex differences in depression: The role of spouse support. In S. Hobfoll (Ed.), *Stress, social support and women* (pp. 69-84). Washington, DC: Hemisphere Publishing.

Veltro, F., Lobrace, S., Storace, F., Maj, M., and Kemali, D. (1990). Prevalence of mental disorders among subjects exposed to seismic phenomena in Naples Province. In C.N. Stefanis, A.D. Rabavilas, C.R. Soldatos, and R. Constantin (Eds.). *Psychiatry: A World Perspective, 4,* 415-419.

Vesti, P., and Kastrup, M. (1992). Psychotherapy for torture survivors. In M. Basoglu (Ed.), *Torture and its consequenses: Current treatment approaches* (pp. 348-362). Cambridge, England: Cambridge University Press.

Wardak, A.W.H. (1988). Neurotic disorders, social support and trauma perception among Ethiopean refugees. Unpublished manuscript. United Kingdom: Department of Psychology, University of Hull, Kingston-Upon-Hull, U.K.

Wardak, A.W.H. (1993). The psychiatric effects of war stress on Afghanistan society. In J. Wilson and B. Raphael (Eds.), *International handbook of traumatic stress syndromes* (pp. 349-364). New York: Plenum Press.

Watson, C. (1990). Psychometric posttraumatic stress disorder measurement techniques: A review. *Psychological Assessment, 2,* 460-469.

Weisaeth, L. (1993). Torture of Norwegian ship's crew: Stress reactions, coping, and psychiatric aftereffects. In J. Wilson and B. Raphael (Eds.), *International handbook of traumatic stress syndromes* (pp. 743-750). New York: Plenum Press.

Weiss, D. (1993). Structured clinical interview techniques. In J. Wilson and B. Raphael (Eds.), *International handbook of traumatic stress syndromes* (pp. 179-188). New York: Plenum Press.

Wells, W. (1974). Group interviewing. In R. Farber (Ed.), *Handbook of marketing research* (pp. 133-146). New York: McGraw-Hill.

Westermeyer, J. and Williams, M. (1998). Three categories of victimization among refugees in a psychiatric clinic. In J.M. Jaranson and M.K. Popkin (Eds.), *Caring for victims of torture* (pp. 61-86). Washington, DC: American Psychiatric Press.

Wheaton, B. (1983). Stress, personal coping resources and psychiatric symptoms: An investigation of an interactive model. *Journal of Health and Social Behavior, 24,* 208-229.

White, M. (1985). Determinants of community satisfaction in Middletown. *American Journal of Community Psychology, 13,* 583-597.

Widgery, R. (1982). Satisfaction with the quality of urban life: A predictive model. *American Journal of Community Psychology, 10,* 37-48.

Wilkinson, C.B. (1983). Aftermath of a disaster: The collapse of the Hyatt Regency hotel skywalks. *American Journal of Psychiatry, 140,* 1134-1139.

Wilson, J. (1988). Understanding the Vietnam veteran. In F. Ochberg (Ed.), *Post-traumatic therapy and victims of violence* (pp. 225-254). New York: Brunner/Mazel.

Wilson, J. (1989). *Trauma, transformation, and healing: An integrative approach to theory, with posttraumatic therapy.* New York: Brunner/Mazel.

Zapf, W. and Glatzer, W. (1987). German social report: Living conditions and subjective well-being, 1978-1984. *Social Indicators Research, 19,* 1-17.

Zatura, A. (1978). *A conceptual guide to measuring quality of life.* Paper presented at the meeting of the American Psychological Association, Toronto, Ontario, August.

Zureik, E., Graff, J., and Ohan, F. (1990). Two years of the *intifada:* A statistical profile of Palestinian victims. *Third World Quarterly, 12,* 97-123.

Index

Page numbers followed by the letter "t" indicate tables.

THE HAWORTH MALTREATMENT AND TRAUMA PRESS
Robert A. Geffner, PhD
Senior Editor

IDENTIFYING CHILD MOLESTERS: PREVENTING CHILD SEXUAL ABUSE BY RECOGNIZING THE PATTERNS OF THE OFFENDERS by Carla van Dam. (2000).

STOPPING THE VIOLENCE: A GROUP MODEL TO CHANGE MEN'S ABU-SIVE ATTITUDES AND BEHAVIORS by David J. Decker. (1999). "A concise and thorough manual to assist clinicians in learning the causes and dynamics of domestic violence." *Joanne Kittel, MSW, LICSW, Yachats, Oregon*

STOPPING THE VIOLENCE: A GROUP MODEL TO CHANGE MEN'S ABU-SIVE ATTITUDES AND BEHAVIORS, THE CLIENT WORKBOOK by David J. Decker. (1999).

BREAKING THE SILENCE: GROUP THERAPY FOR CHILDHOOD SEXUAL ABUSE, A PRACTITIONER'S MANUAL by Judith A. Margolin. (1999). "This book is an extremely valuable and well-written resource for all therapists working with adult survivors of child sexual abuse." *Esther Deblinger, PhD, Associate Professor of Clinical Psychiatry, University of Medicine and Dentistry of New Jersey School of Osteopathic Medicine*

"I NEVER TOLD ANYONE THIS BEFORE": MANAGING THE INITIAL DIS-CLOSURE OF SEXUAL ABUSE RE-COLLECTIONS by Janice A. Gasker. (1999). "Discusses the elements needed to create a safe, therapeutic environment and offers the practitioner a number of useful strategies for responding appropriately to client disclo-sure." *Roberta G. Sands, PhD, Associate Professor, University of Pennsylvania School of Social Work*

FROM SURVIVING TO THRIVING: A THERAPIST'S GUIDE TO STAGE II RECOVERY FOR SURVIVORS OF CHILDHOOD ABUSE by Mary Bratton. (1999). "A must read for all, including survivors. Bratton takes a life-long debilitating disorder and unravels its intricacies in concise, succinct, and understandable language." *Phillip A. Whitner, PhD, Sr. Staff Counselor, University Counseling Center, The Univer-sity of Toledo, Ohio*

SIBLING ABUSE TRAUMA: ASSESSMENT AND INTERVENTION STRAT-EGIES FOR CHILDREN, FAMILIES, AND ADULTS by John V. Caffaro and Alli-son Conn-Caffaro. (1998). "One area that has almost consistently been ignored in the research and writing on child maltreatment is the area of sibling abuse. This book is a welcome and required addition to the developing literature on abuse." *Judith L. Alpert, PhD, Professor of Applied Psychology, New York University*

BEARING WITNESS: VIOLENCE AND COLLECTIVE RESPONSIBILITY by Sandra L. Bloom and Michael Reichert. (1998). "A totally convincing argument. . . . Demands careful study by all elected representatives, the clergy, the mental health and medical professions, representatives of the media, and all those unwittingly involved in this repressive perpetuation and catastrophic global problem." *Harold I. Eist, MD, Past President, American Psychiatric Association*

TREATING CHILDREN WITH SEXUALLY ABUSIVE BEHAVIOR PROBLEMS: GUIDELINES FOR CHILD AND PARENT INTERVENTION by Jan Ellen Burton, Lucinda A. Rasmussen, Julie Bradshaw, Barbara J. Christopherson, and Steven C. Huke. (1998). "An extremely readable book that is well-documented and a mine of valuable 'hands on' information. . . . This is a book that all those who work with sexually abusive children or want to work with them must read." *Sharon K. Araji, PhD, Professor of Sociology, University of Alaska, Anchorage*

THE LEARNING ABOUT MYSELF (LAMS) PROGRAM FOR AT-RISK PARENTS: LEARNING FROM THE PAST—CHANGING THE FUTURE by Verna Rickard. (1998). "This program should be a part of the resource materials of every mental health professional trusted with the responsibility of working with 'at-risk' parents." *Terry King, PhD, Clinical Psychologist, Federal Bureau of Prisons, Catlettsburg, Kentucky*

THE LEARNING ABOUT MYSELF (LAMS) PROGRAM FOR AT-RISK PARENTS: HANDBOOK FOR GROUP PARTICIPANTS by Verna Rickard. (1998). "Not only is the LAMS program designed to be educational and build skills for future use, it is also fun!" *Martha Morrison Dore, PhD, Associate Professor of Social Work, Columbia University, New York, New York*

BRIDGING WORLDS: UNDERSTANDING AND FACILITATING ADOLESCENT RECOVERY FROM THE TRAUMA OF ABUSE by Joycee Kennedy and Carol McCarthy. (1998). "An extraordinary survey of the history of child neglect and abuse in America. . . . A wonderful teaching tool at the university level, but should be required reading in high schools as well." *Florabel Kinsler, PhD, BCD, LCSW, Licensed Clinical Social Worker, Los Angeles, California*

CEDAR HOUSE: A MODEL CHILD ABUSE TREATMENT PROGRAM by Bobbi Kendig with Clara Lowry. (1998). "Kendig and Lowry truly . . . realize the saying that we are our brothers' keepers. Their spirit permeates this volume, and that spirit of caring is what always makes the difference for people in painful situations." *Hershel K. Swinger, PhD, Clinical Director, Children's Institute International, Los Angeles, California*

SEXUAL, PHYSICAL, AND EMOTIONAL ABUSE IN OUT-OF-HOME CARE: PREVENTION SKILLS FOR AT-RISK CHILDREN by Toni Cavanagh Johnson and Associates. (1997). "Professionals who make dispositional decisions or who are related to out-of-home care for children could benefit from reading and following the curriculum of this book with children in placements." *Issues in Child Abuse Accusations*

Order Your Own Copy of
This Important Book for Your Personal Library!

POLITICAL VIOLENCE AND THE PALESTINIAN FAMILY
Implications for Mental Health and Well-Being

_____ in hardbound at $39.95 (ISBN: 0-7890-0898-X)

_____ in softbound at $19.95 (ISBN: 0-7890-1112-3)

COST OF BOOKS_____

OUTSIDE USA/CANADA/
MEXICO: ADD 20%_____

POSTAGE & HANDLING_____
(US: $3.00 for first book & $1.25
for each additional book)
Outside US: $4.75 for first book
& $1.75 for each additional book)

SUBTOTAL_____

IN CANADA: ADD 7% GST_____

STATE TAX_____
(NY, OH & MN residents, please
add appropriate local sales tax)

FINAL TOTAL_____
(If paying in Canadian funds,
convert using the current
exchange rate. UNESCO
coupons welcome.)

☐ **BILL ME LATER:** ($5 service charge will be added)
(Bill-me option is good on US/Canada/Mexico orders only;
not good to jobbers, wholesalers, or subscription agencies.)

☐ Check here if billing address is different from
shipping address and attach purchase order and
billing address information.

Signature_____

☐ **PAYMENT ENCLOSED: $**_____

☐ **PLEASE CHARGE TO MY CREDIT CARD.**

☐ Visa ☐ MasterCard ☐ AmEx ☐ Discover
☐ Diners Club
Account #_____

Exp. Date_____

Signature_____

Prices in US dollars and subject to change without notice.

NAME _____

INSTITUTION _____

ADDRESS _____

CITY _____

STATE/ZIP _____

COUNTRY _____ COUNTY (NY residents only) _____

TEL _____ FAX _____

E-MAIL_____
May we use your e-mail address for confirmations and other types of information? ☐ Yes ☐ No

Order From Your Local Bookstore or Directly From
The Haworth Press, Inc.
10 Alice Street, Binghamton, New York 13904-1580 • USA
TELEPHONE: 1-800-HAWORTH (1-800-429-6784) / Outside US/Canada: (607) 722-5857
FAX: 1-800-895-0582 / Outside US/Canada: (607) 772-6362
E-mail: getinfo@haworthpressinc.com
PLEASE PHOTOCOPY THIS FORM FOR YOUR PERSONAL USE.